FAITH BEYOND BORDERS

(A Study of the Living Religions of the World)

Eternal Water Publications books may be ordered Amazon.com or at:

Eternal Water Publications LLC.
P.O. Box 880373 Port St. Lucie Florida, 34988
www.eternalwaterpublications.com

Due to the dynamic nature of the Internet, any web addresses or links contained in this book may have changed. The views expressed in this work are solely those of the author and do not necessarily reflect the views of the publisher, and the publisher hereby disclaims any responsibility for them.

Any people depicted in stock imagery provided by Istockphoto are models, and such images are being used for illustrative purposes only.

Cover image is provided by ©Istockphoto
Cover design by Miguel Hastings
eBook created with ePubTemplates.com
Available on Kindle and other devices

ISBN: 978-0-692-52483-1

Printed in the United States of America
Printed by Create Space, an Amazon company

Eternal Water Publications

TABLE OF CONTENTS

Dedication

This book is dedicated to my wife Harveybelle and children – Wayne, Alison, and Douglas for their moral and spiritual support in my academic pursuits and Christian ministry. God Bless you always.

Acknowledgements

My profound appreciation is extended to my wife and daughter, Harveybelle and Alison. My wife's critical insight was invaluable for completion of the manuscript. My daughter's editorial astuteness, professionalism in word processing and contextual understanding of the History of Religion is awesome. It has been a time consuming effort for her, but a rewarding one. Thank you Alison.

Leslie Seaton

THE PROLOGUE

I have attempted to write a short history of man's religious faith with special references to five Living Religions of the world. In order to do this I had to begin with man from Creation when he was in communion or fellowship with God. The Genesis account of man reveals that shortly after creation, man lost fellowship with the Divine. Since the fall he has been seeking the path of fellowship back to God. He does this through religious rites and ceremonies. Some of these ceremonies may be used to expiate his sins, others will reveal his gratitude for a world in which he is placed. Still others may show his gregariousness and desire to have fellowship with his fellow man.

The manner in which man expresses his feelings, his emotions toward God can be summed up in the word Faith. Faith is belief. Faith knows no boundaries. The expressions of faith may differ from culture to culture and therefore from religion to religion, but the unchanging principle remains. Faith is firm belief in God. One cannot diagram faith. The expressions of faith are visible, but faith supersedes barriers. The bible is filled with expression or perceptions of faith from the Old Testament to the New Testament. There are people of faith who have made their contributions to our Christian heritage.

Hebrews 11:1-3 discusses faith in these words, "Now, faith is the assurance of things hoped for, the conviction of things not seen. For by it men of old received divine approval. "By faith we understand that the world was created by the word of God so that what is seen was made out of things which do not appear."[1] This definition of faith was deemed suitable by the writer of Hebrews.

It involves hope and trust in the creator who is the ultimate source of our being. This has prompted mankind to adore, pay homage to, worship, and praise the source of his existence. In so doing men and women have offered their gifts and lives to God as a living sacrifice.

---

1. The Holy Bible., The Revised Standard Version. Thomas Nelson Inc. 1972. Hebrews 11: 1-3.

The writer to the Hebrews in Chapter 11:33-39 traces the course of faith from Abel through David and the prophets. Each step of the way he narrates their accomplishments. Thus he writes- "Who through faith conquered kingdoms, enforced justice, received promises, stopped the mouths of lions, quenched raging fires, escaped the edge of the sword, won strength out of weakness, became mighty in war, put foreign armies to flight, women received their dead by resurrection. Some were tortured, refusing to accept release, in order that they might rise again to a better life. Others suffered mocking and scourging, and even chains and imprisonment. They were stoned, they were sawn in two, they went about in skins of sheep and goats, destitute, afflicted, ill-treated; of whom the world was not worthy, wandering over deserts and mountains and in dens and caves of the earth. And all these, though well attested by their faith, did not receive what was promised since God had foreseen something better for us, that apart from us they should not be made perfect."[2]

There is a continuum in the line of Heroes of the faithful. Through their faith they have kept the flame burning. This goes back to the Founder of Christianity on whom the church is built-Jesus Christ, its Savior and Sovereign Lord.

In the great Commission He told the disciples "All authority in heaven and on earth has been given to me. Go therefore and make disciples of all nations, baptizing them in the name of the father, and of the son, and of the Holy Spirit, teaching them to observe all that I have commanded you, and lo, I am with you, to the close of the age."[3]

Of all living religions of the world, only the Christian religion emphasizes the faith of the individual as a vital principle for his religious experience. While the other religions present their codes of ethics emphasizing the dogma and rituals that are embodied as precepts and guiding lights to moral and ethical standards, yet these do not offer man a way to salvation and eternal life here and now, and in the hereafter.

---

2. Ibid., Hebrews 11:33-39.
3. Ibid., Matthew 28: 18 - 20. Chapter 1

Christianity is an exclusive religion. To the Christians, like me, it is the only answer to the longings of man's spirit or soul. Jesus declared that "I am the way, and the truth and the life," in St. John 14:6-7. It is for us to find that way.

Chapter 1

INTRODUCTION TO THEORIES OF RELIGIOUS IDEAS

THEORIES OF RELIGION

The story of God communicating with man, and man's response to God is recorded in the first chapter of Genesis, "In the beginning God created the heavens and the earth." (Genesis 1:1). The literary presentation includes the creation of man. The Cosmogony of Genesis revolves around the mystical number seven. This indicates completeness. It is used to indicate completeness and the orderliness of creation. On the sixth day God created man and woman, giving them authority (dominion) over what he previously created. "So God created man in his own image, in the image of God he created him, male and female he created them, and God blessed them and God said to them, 'Be fruitful and multiply and fill the earth and subdue it, and have dominion over the fish of the sea, and over the birds of the air, and over every living thing that moves upon the earth.' " (Genesis 1: 27-28).

It is not the author's purpose to question the anthropo-morphism in the second account of creation where the Rib Theory of creation (so called by seminarians) appears in the second chapter of Genesis. God caused a "deep sleep to fall upon the man, and while he slept took one of his ribs and closed up the place with flesh, and from the man he made a woman and brought her to the man." (Genesis 2: 21-22). Rather God said "Let us make man…"At God's word all things appeared. The "divine fiat" was responsible for the creation of the world and man. There is no magic in this narrative. God precedes creation. He is the beginning; one may want to call this "Creatio- Ex nihilo" (which is creation out of nothing).

God endowed man with his image. Image does not mean a man was engraved with God's image. Image represents His divine attributes with which man is endowed, such as beauty, order, goodness, kindness, compassion, love, emotion, feelings. The latter three attributes, cause man to cry out for God and he has done so over the years. If there is no connection between man and God then he ends up being lonely indeed.

One will ask – What about man's sin shortly after he discovered himself? A picturesque account of the fall is given in Genesis. Man disobeyed God and fell from his primordial grace. The image in man was not obliterated at the fall. It became defaced. This is one of the reasons why man is constantly thirsting after God. He wants to be re-united with God. Consequently, he seeks ways and means to make connection. The 'ligament' that is fractured is to be reconnected. But only God can repair this relationship. Paul E. Johnson, in Psychology of Religion says; "There is a spark of the divine in man." Is this religion? I think it is. Man is inherently religious. The method by which he displays this religiosity or need for fellowship with God is through his religions.

What is religion? The word religion comes from the Latin term "Religio" which means to bind back. Religion is difficult to define. It is a complex term and consequently one of the broadest terms that language provides. Religion encompasses the largest set of ideas man has conceived as a single collective noun. It covers a vast array of human interests and activities. For the sake of religion, men have earnestly affirmed and contradicted almost every other idea and form of conduct. "In the long history of religion appear chastity, sacred prostitution, feasting and dancing, intoxication and prohibition, dancing and sobriety, sacrifice and the saving of life in orphanages and hospitals, superstition and education, poverty and wealthy endowments, prayer wheels and silent worship, gods and demons, one God and many gods, attempts to escape or to reform the world."[4]

According to Johnson an adequate definition of religion must be general enough to include all types. Religion is response to a sustainer of values. Whether in fear or trust, any action or attitude that recognizes a power able to control values, is religion in the broadest sense. Any sustainer or many who can destroy, give, or withhold what one may need or desire is indicated. A sustainer

---

4. Johnson, Paul E. - Psychology of Religion, Abington Press, New York, Nashville MCMXLV.

may be personal (as a father) or impersonal (as a process), supernatural (a miraculous power), individual as (monotheism) or societal (as in humanism) and institutional (as patriotic devotion to a nation).

"The essentials of religion are (a) a desire for values (b) conscious dependence upon a power which is able to sustain values and (c) a response considered appropriate to realize the values by reference to such a power."[5] Johnson regards this inclusive view as a definition of religion that is not distinctive. Religion must distinguish what is meant from what is not meant, drawing clearly the line between the designated and the undesignated. Religion will need to be distinguished from magic and myth, social customs and organizations, science, philosophy, ethics and aesthetics, though it may have points in common with them.

Religion is personal devotion to an ultimate being; who is believed to offer corrective potentialities for human life through enlarging relationships. Careful observation will reveal that religious devotion is not content for long with the temporal and proximate but insistently seeks the eternal and ultimate. It is natural to respond to a local sustainer of values who may satisfy a desire to give security for the moment, yet every moment points beyond itself, since its fulfillment cannot satisfy for long.

The finite person is ever fragmentary and incomplete. Nothing transient will hold him. There is an endless search (quest) in man for that which will give him ultimate and faithful response to his deepest need. "Other hungers may be satisfied with food at home and if supply is constant; a person may grow fat and lazy with this security, but a religious longing of ultimate concern is not so. For this is a hunger that nothing will satisfy and no material supply will give the answer sought. The ultimate quest is for a BEING who confronts me in a living relationship as I search for him. I am determined to meet THOU; for nothing less will give my life ultimate significance."[6]

There are some religious seekers who believe that the creative

---

5. Ibid., p. 48.
6. Ibid., p. 49.

potentialities of life are to be found in the meeting of I, and THOU. To reverence another person is to meet him as THOU with honest appreciation of his worth and dignity as a creative center of valuing experience. To meet a finite person in this way is not to make him the ultimate THOU, for he is local and transient in relation to me. Religious meeting is therefore interpersonal.

Religion therefore has its substance in the realm of personality. Personality is a unique center of individual life striving for goals through dynamic relationships. Not all these goals have ultimate meaning; many are sought for immediate satisfaction. As each goal is reached it births other goals. In the ongoing search for a goal beyond goals and a relationship beyond relations, a person may develop the ultimate concern for religion. This is where faith in God plays a dominant role in man's existence. He has asked the following questions. Who am I? Where did I come from? What will I be? Is there a life after death? Man has a desire to place order over chaos, and perceive with certainty why certain events happen in life and to imagine what occurs beyond the border of death. So, the prospect of a hidden deity imposing his structured will on earth is an appealing one. "Man can steal back a modicum of control through appeasement of the gods through prayers, sacrifices, piety and charity."[7]

Religion comes naturally to most of us. It inspires resonating themes in wonderful music and fabulous works of art such as good vs. evil, right and wrong, and strength through faith. Even in today's mostly secular society we are brought up on stories and fables inherited from our forefathers. There is a fascinating array of beliefs. The study of religion reveals that a surprising number, place emphases on one creator God, although Buddhism does not acknowledge a god at all. "Before religion can work, reason and rationality must be suspended. Seemingly preposterous claims of miracles and meetings with God have been made by the founders of great religions including Judaism, Christianity and Islam. However such occurrences have been vouchsafed as genuine by millions of people in the past two thousand years."[8]

---

7. Harrington, Karen – The History of Religion, Barnes and Noble, 1998. p. 9.
8. Ibid., p. 9.

Some people believe that a God launched the moon in orbit or slowed down the passage of the sun to make a day. Their faith just like their God is intangible, but remains a cornerstone of their existence. Harrington maintained that man's evolution remains a perplexing subject, despite many educated guesses and happy archeological accidents.

All religions have at their apex, a Supreme Being whether it is in Africa, Australia, the Far East, the Middle East, North America, Central America, South America, and the Islands of the Seas. Even in areas where there are thousands of different tribes speaking various languages, and holding contrasting beliefs, this is true. In all religions of the undeveloped world, the religious tradition is oral. There are many essays or papers to study that debate about African religion in particular. It appears that tribes acknowledge a supreme being although, not one that is necessarily involved in human affairs.[9]

In North America the Native American's observe Totem-ism. Australian aborigines offer sacrifices to the Superior being. The Aztecs of South America, practiced mass human sacrifice. The Incas worshipped the Sun God and Inti the Creation God.

Dr. Paul Hutchinson in 'How Mankind Worships' writes; "Endless are the forms man's religion has taken. The names of his gods and goddesses will never be completely catalogued. The rituals through which he has sought protection or blessing run the gamut from the horrible to the sublime. The explanations of his rites may fill ten thousand volumes, and many of them disagree violently. Such young and fascinating sciences as Anthropology, Archaeology and Paleontology are constantly uncovering new evidence concerning the life of our Paleolithic Ancestors. The evidence brings to light infinite variations, but on one thing it agrees. Man is a religious being."[10]

In our contemporary world while there are many religions. By far the most influential, reckoning by the extent of their followings

---

9. Ibid., page 17.
10. Luce, Henry R., - Editor In Chief, The World's Great Religions, Time Life Incorporated, New York, 1957. p. 1.

are; Hinduism, Buddhism, Judaism, Islam, and Christianity. Paul Hutchinson lists the six most influential religions as Hinduism, Buddhism- the religions of the Chinese, then Islam, Judaism, and Christianity. "The affinities between some of them are many, the differences are also many. In some instances they are fundamentally the same. But all of them obviously have supplied answers to many of the great questions roused in every human mind by the mystery of life, all have brought strength to bear its sorrows, all have shed light on the path of conduct, all have furnished assurance in the presence of death. They have done this with varying effectiveness."[11]

Hutchinson concedes that as a Christian he would not conceal his belief that Christianity has been the most effective of all religions; yet all have brought answers to men's prayers. If it were not so the others would not be living religions. They all deserve our study and our respectful understanding. "Buddhism came out of Hinduism and Hinduism in its bewildering variety. In some, the same primitive village worship elements from which the religion emerged, aspects are still present. Mohammed explicitly acknowledged his indebtedness to Judeo-Christian sources." For the Jewish and Christian faith, the bible is a superb record of the way in which out of a nomad beginning, influences by the civilizations of the Nile and the Middle East, Jews were challenged and at times seduced by the deities of the land. The Hebrew Tribes which settled in Palestine finally came to worship the majestic, yet forgiving monotheistic God of the prophets and Jesus.[12]

All Religions trace back; all have in their lore, likeness to the love of other Faiths. "Jewish and Christian scholars, reading the 4,000 year old Babylonian epic of Gilgamesh find in it striking parallels to the Genesis story of Noah, with an Ark covered by pitch, the rain, and the sending out of the raven and dove. The Ark landing on a mountain-simply added evidence of the extent to which Hebrew culture emerged out of, and was influenced by, that of the Tigris and Euphrates Valley. When Greece was overrun by the Roman legions, the Gods and Goddesses (of which Homer sang) were renamed and became a part of the Roman Pantheon."[13]

---

11. Ibid., p. 1.
12. Ibid., p. 1.
13. Ibid., p. 1.

Chapter 2

THEORIES OF RELIGIOUS IDEAS

THE COVENANT GOD

Noah saw the destruction that Yahweh would send upon his people. He built an Ark to withstand the flood that Yahweh would send upon the earth because of the sinfulness of the people. After forty days and nights the flood subsided. Noah and his family and a pair of animals of each kind survived. After this Noah offered his sacrifices of Thanksgiving to Yahweh (Jehovah). A covenant was established between Yahweh and Noah. This embraced Noah; his family, and every living creature with him. "I will establish my covenant with you and never again shall all flesh be cut off by the waters of a flood." "I set my bow in the cloud and it shall be a sign of the covenant between me and the earth" (Genesis 9:15, &13). The covenant with Noah was sealed with a promise. "While the earth remains, seed time and harvest, cold and heat, summer and winter, day and night shall not cease"(Genesis 8:22).

Abraham played a very important part in the Covenant theory. Indeed Canaanite religion began with Abraham. He has become the father of the Jewish Nation, because he proved to be a man of implicit faith in Jehovah. In Genesis Chapter 22 Abraham is told by God to take his only legitimate son Isaac to Mount Moriah to offer him as a sacrifice.

This he did, but in the act of sacrificing Isaac he was forbidden by God's Angel "Do not lay your hand on this lad or do any such thing to him, for now I know that you fear God, seeing you have not withheld your son, your only son from me"(Genesis 22:12). A substitute was provided in the ram caught in a thicket. Abraham called the name of the place Jehovah Jireh (The Lord will provide).

Abraham was given a blessing and a promise, by the Angel of the Lord. His descendants would be multiplied as the stars of heaven and as the sands on the sea shore (Genesis 22:17). The sign of the covenant was to be the circumcision of Abraham and Isaac, a practice, which is still carried out on all Jewish boys when they are eight days old.

Abraham arranged a marriage for Isaac to his cousin Rebekah. She would give birth to Jacob and Esau. Jacob went on to father 12 sons the heads of the twelve tribes. Abraham however, died at the age of 175 and was buried with his wife Sarah. Abraham was renowned for his hospitality. So great was his love for man that he stood at the door of his tent to urge guests inside. "Even today, Rabbis point to Abraham as an example for Jews to follow and by tradition everyone is welcome at the dinner table, particularly the festive meals"[14] Harrelson regards this period as Israel's Primeval History.

Judaism really began to take shape with the story of the Exodus. If Abraham became the father of the Hebrew people, Moses became the great law giver. After meeting with God he passed on a series of laws which resulted in a Canonization of Hebrew laws and practices. Under the Josephites, during Egyptian bondage, the Pharaoh felt that the Israelites developed into a great threatening force. Consequently he ordered all the male Israelite babies to be killed or thrown into the River Nile.

The Hebrew woman Jochebed gave birth to a fine healthy boy in Egypt. She left the baby in a water-tight basket made from bull rushes in the shallows of the Nile. A short distance away, the baby's sister waited and watched. Pharaoh's daughter came down to the river to bathe and the noble woman found Moses. Miriam seized the moment. She dashed down, offering to help the Pharaoh's daughter find an Israelite wet nurse for the baby. Moments later, she produced Jochebed. Unknown to the Egyptian on- lookers, the mother and her son were reunited. The dramatic events following his birth in 1593 BC were merely preparation for Moses' later life. Moses was the leader who spearheaded the Exodus.

THE EXODUS

The Exodus marks the high water mark in Israel's history and

---

14. Harrelson, Walter., Interpreting the Old Testament, Holt, Rinehart, Winston Inc., New York,1964. p 43.

religion. A significant aspect of this is the Passover. The Lord said to Moses; "Consecrate to me all the first born. Whatever is the first born to open the womb among the people help, both of men and of beast is mine" (Exodus 13:1). God sent plagues on the Egyptians in retribution for not releasing His people. Time and time again, Moses, with God's help, instigated ten plagues on Pharaoh and the Egyptians. The first- turning the waters of the Nile into blood. Then came frogs, lice, flies, disease, boils, hail, locusts and darkness. The last was the most terrible, the death of every Egyptian first born, while the Israelites first born were saved-thus the term Passover. After this the Pharaoh finally acquiesced and the Israelites left Egypt. The Egyptian army was in hot pursuit but Moses saved his followers by miraculously parting the waters of the Red Sea, leading his people across, and leaving waves to crash down on the pursuers.

For years it was accepted that at God's bidding Moses wrote the first five books of the Hebrew Bible (known as the Pentateuch). Moses is responsible for recording the Ten Commandments found in Exodus 20:1-7. For this, he is acclaimed the lawgiver and the father of Jewish Laws. The Ten Commandments revealed God's ideas for Covenant with Israel. They read as follows:

- I am the Lord your God, you shall have no other Gods before me;

- You shall not make for yourself a graven image, nor any likeness of anything that is in heaven or that is on earth beneath, or that is in the waters under the earth; You shall not bow down to them, nor serve them for I the Lord your God am a jealous God;

- You shall not take the name of the Lord in vain, for the Lord God will not hold him guiltless who takes his name in vain;

- Remember the Sabbath day to keep it Holy;

- Honor your mother and father that your days may be long in the land which your God gives you;

- You shall not kill;

- You shall not commit adultery;

- You shall not steal;

- You shall not bear false witness against your neighbor;

- You shall not covet your neighbor's house, or anything that belongs to him.

The Hebrew legal system depends on these Commandments. These Ten Commandments have influenced the legal system in the Western World. The two sections both Apodictic and Casuistic, still guide and govern the Democratic systems of the world today. Apodictic Law refers to divine commands while Casuistic Law is case law which has a series of statements, each linked to its coinciding punishment if violated. In fact the Old Testament is home to three aspects of Hebraic Law Codes; The Covenant Code or Law found in Exodus, The Deuteronomic Code found in Deuteronomy and the Priestly code found in Leviticus, Numbers and parts of Exodus.

The period in Israel's history during the desert wanderings toward the Promised Land as well as the period of The Judges was not without its religious flaws. Yahwehism witnessed some adaptations, accommodations, syncretism and assimilation. Israelites were exposed to Pantheism and Polytheism. How could Yahwehism remain pure with a people who saw the success of others who were blessed by their gods? Hebrew faith turned to the worship of other cults, images, and gods and in so doing they broke the Covenant by turning away to heathen or 'pagan' gods.

The stories of Joshua and Gideon illustrate struggles with this form of apostasy. Joshua had to remind his people about Yahwehistic loyalty and faithfulness. Joshua gathered all of the tribes of Israel at Shechem and summoned the elders, the heads, the judges and the officers of Israel, and they presented themselves before God. He then gave them his farewell message. "Now therefore fear the Lord and serve him in sincerity and in faithfulness, put away the gods which your fathers served beyond the river and in Egypt and serve the Lord. And if you be unwilling to serve the Lord, choose this day whom you will serve-but as for me and my house, we will serve the Lord."[15]

---

15. The Holy Bible, The Revised Standard Version, Joshua 24: 14 – 15

During the period of The Judges when 'every man did what was pleasing in his own eyes,' Israel's religion degenerated into a state of apostasy. Israel forsook the Lord for Baal and Asherah. On every hill and under every green tree there was a god for them to worship.

It was Gideon who destroyed the altar of Baal;after he had built an altar to the Lord and called it, "the Lord is Peace." That same night the Lord said to him, "Take your father's bull, the second bull, seven years old and pull down the altar of Baal which your father has and cut down the Asherah that is beside it, and build an altar to the Lord your God on the top of the stronghold with stones laid in due order, then take the second bull, and offer it as a burnt offering with the wood of Asherah, which you shall cut down. So Gideon took ten men of his servants and did as the Lord had told him."[16]

It must be noted that Asherah was a representative of the Fertility goddess of Canaan. Baal was the principal Canaanite god. Gideon is the first of Israel's leaders to attack outright the worship of Baal. Gideon's attack on Baalism was quite different from that of Elijah. Gideon was claiming for Yahweh those powers assigned by others to Baal.

---

16. Ibid., Judges 6:25 – 27.

Chapter 3

CHIEF FEATURES OF CANAANITE RELIGION AND HOW IT COMPARES TO ISRAEL'S FAITH AND PRACTICE

The alphabet and other writings contain myths and epics telling of the gods of Canaan and their relation to one another. The Chief god of the Pantheon at Ugaret was El. Listed below are several key deities:

1. Êl. He and his wife Asherah lived at the source of two rivers, somewhat removed from daily governance of the Cosmos, but available to settle disputes and to hear appeals from the other gods.

2. Baal is the male deity, the god of the Heavens, the giver of fertility to the soil, to man, and to beast. Baal actually won victory over Mot annually with the aid of his sister and consort Anath.[17]

3. Yam the God of the seas, and the underwater ocean.

4. Mot the God of Summer, drought and death.

5. Anath represents the triumph of life over death in the rhythm of the seasons.

Canaanite religion was oriented toward the soil and fertility, toward the maintenance and reproduction of life. There was a plurality of gods, although Baal held the Chief place among the gods. The worship of Baal involved the making of sacrifice of fruit, grain, animals, the offering of prayers, and the celebration of Baal's powers in great ritual cults that recounted the story of the god's triumph. The religion of Canaan resembled that of the other peoples of the Ancient world in many aspects. "The religion of Canaan was not necessarily crude and debased."

On the contrary it probably had much of beauty and religious power, meeting man's needs in an agricultural religious

---

17. Harrelson, Walter., Interpreting the Old Testament, p. 3 (Harrelson).

community. The Israelites apparently found Canaanite religious practice and understandings almost irresistibly attractive. The fundamental flaw in Canaanite religion lay in its providing too easy a path for man to secure the favor of the gods. Religion moreover was the instrument of the people in maintaining society. Israelite religion drew heavily upon the religious traditions and practices of Canaan. That which prevented the Israelites from simply adapting the religion of Canaan was the conviction that Yahweh their God was best known in the events of their past history and in their present historical trials and accomplishments.

However the Israelites quickly adapted from the Canaanites the practice of offering sacrifices of grain and fruit. These offerings were the gifts to Yahweh who had led them out of Egypt and provided the rich land as their inheritance. The festivals of barley harvest (Pentecost) and fruit harvest (Tabernacles) were either adapted from the Canaanites or, as in the case of the Passover, adapted to the agricultural situation. The first and third of these festivals became times of holy remembrance of Yahweh's past deeds of salvation as well as times of celebration of the gift of food for the coming year. The people constructed altars which bore some semblance to the Canaanite models. At first this met with some resistance. The garments of the Priests probably resembled the prevailing Canaanite styles. "In general, the worship was modified to assign Yahweh, the powers that in Canaan were associated with Baal and the other Gods of the Canaanite Pantheon."[18]

During the reign of Ahab, Jezebel his wife introduced the worship of the high god Baal – Melkart into Israel from Phoenicia. Jezebel took an active part in the government of Israel (1Kings 21). She supported at the state expense, hundreds of priests- prophets of Baal. A determined effort was made in Ahab's reign to transform the religious allegiance of the people. Ahab himself remained a worshipper of Yahweh, but he probably acquiesced to his wife's desires to transform the worship of Yahweh into the worship of the fertility god Baal. Ahab built a house for Baal in the capital city and made an Asherah for the shrine. This was a decorated pole or

---

18. Ibid., p. 154.

outright image of the Deity.

The prophet Elijah denounced the worship of Baal. He entered a contest with Baal's priests on Mount Carmel to prove who the God in Israel was; Baal or Yahweh (1 Kings 18)? First he called for a drought (1 Kings 17). Secondly he announced that Yahweh and Baal were to contend on Mount Carmel to answer this question (1Kings 18). The true God would end the drought. Would Baal end the drought or would Yahweh? Would fire consume the sacrifice? Would Yahweh send rain?

THE DRAMA ON MT CARMEL TOOK THIS FORM:

1. Elijah appears before Ahab and calls for a convocation upon Mt. Carmel where Elijah alone will confront the prophets of Baal and Asherah.

2. Ahab gathers the people.

3. The contest is agreed upon. The priests of Baal prepare their bull for sacrifice and began their prayers to Baal that he consume the sacrifice on the altar. Prayers, dancing, mutilation of the body, frenzy before Baal occurs: but is to no avail. Elijah taunts the priests as their efforts continue throughout the day. But no one answers and no one heeds.

4. Elijah demands a radical decision then and there on the part of the people, and the king. There can be no continuation of this mixture of allegiance to Yahweh and to Baal. Either one or the other is God.

5. Elijah repairs the old altar on Mount Carmel that had been in disrepair for some time. He poured water on it and the offering and prays that Yahweh consume the sacrifice, and it is immediately consumed. The people respond with a cry "Yahweh, he is God."[19]

6. Elijah slaughters the humiliated priests of Baal, sends Ahab to continue with his festivity before Yahweh. Then he goes further up the slopes of Carmel to pray for rain.

---

19. The Holy Bible, Revised Standard Version, 1st Kings 18:39.

7.   The servant brings report that a tiny cloud is visible over the Mediterranean to the west. Elijah summons Ahab to go quickly to Jezreel, the prophet running before the chariot all the way to Jezreel.

The religious apostasy and assimilation of Baalism did not end at Mt. Carmel. Israel's sins were also condemned by other prophets. Hosea applied the metaphor of his wife's unfaithfulness (harlotry) to Israel's unfaithfulness to Yahweh. The husband who had lavished all good things upon the bride Israel has come to the point beyond which he will no longer tolerate such an Israel. He condemns the feasts, New moons, Sabbath. These festivals were certainly celebrations of unfaithfulness. Israel had abandoned the worship of Yahweh for that of Baal, even though the people still name Yahweh's name.

Hosea still spoke of God's *Chesed* (loving kindness) or rule of Yahweh over Israel. The attack then is upon practices which revealed to the prophet that Israel had forsaken Yahweh even though she would deny this vehemently. The feast days of Yahweh had become feast days of Baal. "It can be implied that the worship of Baal and that of Yahweh simply exist alongside of one another with many of the people finding nothing inconsistent in this fact"[20] (also seen in Elijah's entreaty in 1 Kings 18:21). "Some of the people in Israel may simply have viewed this attitude eminently sensible and practical."[21]

For Hosea the worship of Yahweh must not involve such practices as fertility cults. Hosea promises devastation of the land as punishment for Israel's apostasy. However, Yahweh will turn again to the "faithless wife" Israel. He will have mercy and show love. Hosea abhors the use of cultic formulas by means of which the people summoned the aid of Baal or Yahweh, to bring fruitfulness to the land. The cultic formula involved the invocation of the sown grain, the vines and the fruit and olive trees to produce the fruit of the coming season. They turn to the earth, calling upon the earth to provide its strength and support. The earth addresses the heavens, seeking rain and sun in order that it may produce. The

---

20. Harrelson, Walter Interpreting the Old Testament, p. 323.
21. Ibid., p. 323.

latter in turn appeals to Baal- the lord of heavens and fertility, thus invoking the powers of the god, and each agent of the deity does its part so that man may have food and drink for the coming season.

The prophet Hosea laid before Israel the most basic element in biblical faith. God's people have hope in His divine love. If God (Yahweh) does not act for the salvation of His people out of His love and mercy towards them, then there is no hope at all. Israel's deed of righteousness and faithfulness can be enacted, when they respond to God's love. Israel can come before Yahweh with the most precious gifts of; acknowledging His Lordship and confession. But man's life depends not only upon an understanding of the divine relationship in man's historical existence. Man's life has its rhythms as does the life of the earth in Divine Providence. "The church in subsequent centuries has also drawn into its religious life many elements from the religions of fertility. The priestly tradition (P) has given great prominence to Yahweh's granting of fertility to the soil and to mankind in Genesis 1. Hosea and other prophets have helped to provide the means by which the nature religions could make their proper contribution to Israelites faith, and its religious practices and understanding."[22]

Baalism also flourished during the reign of Manasseh. "The worship of the sun, moon and stars spread in Judah."[23] The worship of the god Milkom (the Ammonites deity) was practiced by those who called themselves worshipers of Yahweh. This religious corruption was the cause of Zephaniah's, Isaiah's, and Jeremiah's attack on continuing to place elements of other deities alongside the worship of Yahweh. Zephaniah's basic complaint was that men of Judah expected neither good nor evil from Yahweh. He describes the coming day of Yahweh with vigor and horror. Yahweh has appointed a day, indeed a cult day, which isn't a day for renewal of life and blessing. God will confront his people with darkness and gloom, not light and rejoicing. This will signal a complete end of God's people. Yahweh will come to "sweep away all things from the face of the earth."[24] He calls God's faithless people to assemble for the judgment of the covenant God. Israel is

---

22. Ibid., p. 326.
23. The Holy Bible, Revised Standard Version, 2nd Kings 21:2-9.
24. Ibid., Zephaniah 1:2.

called to return to Yahweh, to seek God who alone can deliver her in the coming of calamity. 'Before it is too late, let those declare themselves who will return to Yahweh, in humility and righteousness.'[25]

Zephaniah offered this possibility of hope to those who would even at the last moment declare themselves to be faithful adherents of the covenant God. Zephaniah continued the prophetic tradition of Amos and of Isaiah. He spoke with severity against the faithless covenant community, depicting Yahweh's worldwide judgment upon the nations. Zion, the center of Yahweh's activity will nonetheless bring life and blessings or judgment to some among foreign people. He stood more closely with Jerusalem cultic tradition than Amos, Hosea, Isaiah, and Micah. In his exhortations no condemnation of sacrifices is heard.

But the day of Yahweh which he described is precisely the Day of Judgment which the throngs in the temple would have understood to mean the renewal of Yahweh's favor and blessing in the New Year celebration. The cultic day is for Zephaniah a time of complete devastation of Israel and the nations.

Isaiah however presents Israelite faith in its most profound expression. The period of Isaiah's own lifetime (740-700 B.C.) is filled with religious corruption. He introduced into Judah the classic prophetic tradition already apparent in the North through the work of Amos and Hosea. Isaiah's prophecy was true to the vision in the Temple.[26]Yahweh surrounded by the heavenly host, is making plans for bringing judgment upon the faithless people. Seraphim (winged creatures probably of mixed form, part animal, part bird, part human) hover over the divine throne, waiting to do God's bidding and also proclaiming the holiness of Yahweh, "Isaiah has done more than any other prophet to elucidate and develop the meaning of God's holiness."[27] God shows Himself holy in righteousness. Yahweh the holy God appears before sinful men. Isaiah provides a strong ethical dimension to the Israelites understanding of holiness. He is not of course, the first to do so,

---

25. Ibid., Zephaniah 2: 3.
26. Harrelson, Interpreting the Old Testament. p. 232.
27. Harrelson, Walter., Interpreting the Old Testament, p. 232.

but he emphasizes as no predecessor had done, the connection between Yahweh's awe-inspiring terror and splendor and the righteousness of his deeds and purposes.

Isaiah was commissioned to proclaim judgment upon Israel for her sins. He said Judah's cities would be wasted, her people cut off from the land. If even so much as a tenth of the population should be spared, that one tenth would also be ravaged. But Yahweh would not completely destroy the "stump". The prophet of Israel had a word of final hope in Yahweh and in the fulfillment of Yahweh's purpose through Israel – "The Holy Seed."[28] Isaiah never gave up completely upon God. From the household of David, he predicted God's agent would come to lead the people in the reconstruction of land and people in a coming day.

Jeremiah echoed the coming of a New Covenant, which would be written not on tablets of stone but in the inward part -- the heart. But the day of Yahweh, which he describes, is precisely that Day of Judgment. Like Zephaniah he prophesied that the throngs in the Temple would have understood the renewal of Yahweh's favor and blessing on the New Year Celebration.

Jeremiah was born in Anathoth at about the time the young Josiah came to the throne in Judah (640-639 B.C). He dedicated his early ministry against infidelity of God's people to the demands of the Covenant Faith. He probably found the reforms of Josiah, carried through in 621 B.C., to be a sign of great hope. Jeremiah never ceased to lay before Judah, the divine word. He was to witness the first deportation of Judeans into Babylonian exile (577 B.C.), the efforts of Zedekiah to maintain order in the troubled state during the subsequent years, until the city fell in 586 B.C., and the actual destruction of Jerusalem.

Jeremiah engaged in a "preaching mission" in support of the reforms of Josiah. He sought for the centralization of worship in Jerusalem, which resulted in the hostility of the men of Anathoh against him, and the consequent loss of the local sanctuary at which, perhaps his own priestly family officiated.

The covenant at Sinai was not Jeremiah's ultimate aim. He was

---

28. The Holy Bible, Revised Standard Version, Isaiah 6.

not merely promising life and security to Judah in return for support of Josiah's reform. He saw signs of idolatry and faithlessness all around "He threatens coming ruin to Judah if there is not a radical amendment of her ways. Jeremiah can be content with no purification of worship that does not rest upon radical repentance."[29]

He selected the potter's wheel to describe what Yahweh could do with Israel. 'As the clay is in the potter's hand, so is Israel in Yahweh's hand.' Yahweh will deal with Israel, shaping her to his purpose, making a fresh start with her, if he chooses. Yahweh is the sovereign Lord of the Nations. He uses them to accomplish his design, his purpose, as the potter uses the clay. The fulfillment of the divine covenant, the placing of the Torah in the inward parts of man so that obedience becomes as natural as life or breathing is the hallmark of Jeremiah's prophecy.

---

29. Harrelson, Walter., p. 269.

Chapter 4

JUDAISM

Judaism belongs to the same family of religion as Christianity and Islam. The ethos of each faith is the same, that there is one all-powerful God and compassionate creator. "Despite age–old conflicts between them, these three different routes to God are remarkably alike. All three religions demand similar standards of behavior. To each, although for different reasons, Jerusalem is a hallowed city."[30]

The Jewish religion, Judaism dates back at least 3000 years. The feeling of Judaism is different from the other monotheistic religions. More than a system of beliefs, this religion exudes a sense of identity - a tradition that binds families and fellow Jews together, no matter what. This deep-rooted allegiance has kept the faith alive during a history of unprecedented trauma.

Judaism began with the creation narrative. God created heaven and earth, water, and animals. On the sixth day he created man and woman. Together they fell from grace. God punished them with hard work for men, painful childbearing for women, and death for all. The first man to feature in Hebrew literature, in the flood story, was Noah. God decided to punish man for his evil ways with a flood. Noah being found by God to be the only righteous man alive was told to build an ark and take his family and one pair of all the world's animals on board. It rained for 40 days and nights and the waters destroyed all living things except those on Noah's ark. When the flood subsided the ark came to rest on Mt Ararat. "All the world's population can trace their line back to Noah, the grandson of Methuselah who died in the year of the flood at the age of 969 years."[31]

The second prominent man in Judaism is Abram (Abraham). A descendant of Noah's son Shem, he was wealthy and good. He lived with his wife Sarai and nephew Lot in the great city Ur in

---

30. Harrington, Karen., The History of Religion, Barnes and Noble, 1998, .41.
31. Ibid., p.42.

Babylonia around 1700 B.C. and was the first Patriarch so he features prominently in the Jewish faith.

At the instigation of Abraham's father Terah, the idol maker, the family left UR to follow a nomadic life. God urged Abraham to go to Canaan where he would found a great nation. God promised he would be known as Abraham (the father of the multitude). Sarah urged Abraham to father a child by her Egyptian maid Hagar and so Ishmael was born, and destined to figure prominently in Islam's history. It was not until Abraham was 99 - that he and his wife produced their own child, a son called Isaac.

God commanded Abraham to sacrifice Isaac. Father and son went up into the mountain where Abraham prepared the altar, built a pyre, bound his son, and was about to wield the knife to kill the boy when God's angel intervened. Abraham had not flinched. Such was his faith in the will of God. To reward such unquestioning loyalty God made a covenant with Abraham. "Because you have done this and have not withheld your son, your favored one, I will bestow my blessing upon you and make your descendants as numerous as the stars in heaven."[32] The sign of the Covenant was to be circumcision of Abraham and Isaac, a practice which continued to be carried out on all Jewish boys when they are eight days old.

Abraham arranged a marriage for Isaac to his cousin Rebekah, who would later give birth to Jacob and Esau. Abraham died at age 175 and was buried at the same site as his wife Sarah. Jacob fathered 12 sons who became leaders of a dozen different tribes of Israel.

Another important aspect of Judaism is the Exodus - a dramatic event in which Moses and his brother confronted Pharaoh, asking him to let the Israelites go. For most of his life, Moses was a humble shepherd, until God spoke to him through a burning bush, calling him to free his people from Egyptian slavery. When the purpose of his mission was denied time and time again, Moses with God's help instigated ten plagues. The last being the most terrible, the death of every Egyptian first born, finally convinced

---

32. The Holy Bible, Revised Standard Version, Genesis 22: 16 - 17.

Pharaoh to release the Israelites. The Egyptian army took hot pursuit at their leaving. Moses saved his followers by parting the waters of the Red Sea (the sea of reeds), leading his people across and leaving the waves to crash down upon the Egyptians.

The journey to the Promised Land was arduous. Moses was plagued with endless complaints from the Israelites. There were even attempted coups to remove Moses from power. Moses felt himself to be a weak man. He was also over 80 when he went to free the slaves. Through an outburst of anger Moses lost the opportunity to enter the Promised Land. God was unrelenting and condemned him to die in the desert.

THE WORD OF GOD

Moses received the Ten Commandments on Mount Sinai and carved them in stone tablets, which were placed in an ark. The ark accompanied the Hebrew people on their wanderings until it finally came to rest in the Temple in Jerusalem, and vanished about the 6th century B.C. The Commandments in Exodus 20: 1-17 are followed by other statements on conduct, which would separate the Old Testament God from the New. For years it was accepted that at God's bidding, Moses wrote the first five books of the Hebrew Bible – Genesis, Exodus, Leviticus, Numbers, Deuteronomy. These are known as the Pentateuch.

THE SHEMA

Shema "Yisroel Adonai Elohenu Adonai Echod" Hear O Israel, the Lord our God, the Lord is one. These tremendous words, uttered to the Jewish people by Moses as the spokes-person of God, mark a sharp dividing line in the world's religions. They created a new concept of God. "Not only Judaism but Christianity and Islam teach one should adhere to strict Monotheism. That is what sets them apart from the world's other major concepts of divine and human order i.e., Oriental religions and Greek thought."[33]

In Judaism as God is one, so is life. Every part of it must be

---

33. Luce, Henry R., Editor in Chief, Time Life Inc. The World's Great Religions., p. 133.

sanctified. As life is one, so is man. There is no division between the evil represented by body and the good represented by the soul; for both must sense God. Ideally, the table must be an altar, the home a house of God, the market place an expression of justice. That is why the religious Jew moves through life on a round of blessings.

Judaism sees man as a paradox. He is a handful of dust, but he also carries the divine spark. He is fashioned in the image of God and this means above all that he has freedom. He lives in the perpetual crisis of free will, faced at every moment with choice between good and evil. Judaism holds that man, being man, cannot escape sin. But Adam's fall is not seen as a stain automatically transmitted – as in the orthodox Christian concept of original sin. Adam's fall is seen rather as a fault again and again repeated because of man's human weakness through loving God, and by striving to imitate him. Man must also love his fellow human beings. When love goes beyond the law or mercy beyond justice, it is an ancient argument. The strict Jewish answer is that love and the law must be one and the same.[34]

In Jewish law, a Jew does not cease being a Jew simply because he lapses from religious observance. Anyone born of a Jewish mother is a Jew. Jewish ritual is relatively un-dramatic. Its synagogues are without graven images. Its greatest image is an idea, the idea of the one living God. The Jews believe when God elected them to be, "The Chosen People", he gave them special responsibilities rather than privileges. He appointed Israel to be His suffering servant to bring His word to all peoples of the world.

Jewish and Christian Theologians believe that the Jews' mission till history ends is to bear witness against idolatry, against man made gods, which are made not only of stone and bronze, but also of false ideas. The hope is that all may one day learn and never forget that "the Lord our God is one." Jesus, in his dialogue with the scribe who inquired of him 'Which commandment is the first?' reiterated this familiar phrase from a second commandment of equal significance. "You shall love your neighbor as yourself."[35]

---

34. Ibid., p 133.
35. Ibid., p. 133.

JEWISH LAW

Halakhah is the Jewish law encompassing everything from criminal and civil law to morals and ethics. It is over attitudes in the Halakhah that the Jewish faith split. Orthodox Jews accept the law and rabbinical authority.

In the 18th century, liberal Judaism arose in Europe to question age-old traditions and encourage constructive criticism of the Torah and the Talmud. It was given continuity by reform on progressive Judaism which plays down elements like the expectation of a Messiah and the desire to return to the Holy Land. Reformed Jews offer equal opportunity to women during worship, while worshippers in the Orthodox Synagogues are separated by sex. Conservative Jews steer a middle course. There are also Hasidic Jews who try to reach God through ecstatic prayer.

THE TORAH AND THE TALMUD

To a Jewish male, the quest to know the Torah, begins in boyhood and never ends. One verse in the ethics of the Fathers sums up the Jewish attitude to the Bible "Turn it, and turn it, for everything is in it. Contemplate it and grow old and gray over it, and do not stir from it. You can follow no better course than this."[36]

The Talmud is comprised of two different forms of writing; the first, is the Mishnah, and the second is the Gemara. The Mishna is the tradition which was committed to paper in about A.D. 200, following the martyrdom of Rabbi Akiba. It was eventually marshaled into six sections, each dealing with different aspects of life. There was one each; for agriculture, festival days, marriages and divorce, the law, the temple sacrifices and ritual purification. There are two Talmud's, one for Babylonia and the other for Palestine (Jerusalem). The first being three times longer than the second, is generally considered the most cumulative. Both are written in a mixture of Hebrew and Aramaic. Attempts to codify the contents of The Talmud's to make them less academic and more accessible have been made over the years.

---

36. Karen Harrington., p. 51.

NEV'IM (THE PROPHETS)

After the Torah comes the section of the Hebrews bible - the Prophets or Nev'im. Nev'im is divided into eight books. It is probably the oldest detailed narrative known to man, which focuses on the former prophets, Judges and Kings. The books included are; Joshua, Judges, Samuel and Kings and the latter prophets; Isaiah, Jeremiah, and Ezekiel. Then follows the Minor Prophets, - all responsible for relaying God's message to the Israelites.

KETUBIM (OTHER PARTS OF THE JEWISH WRITINGS)

The third section of the Hebrew Bible is the "Writings" or Ketubim, which includes the Psalms, Proverbs, Job, the Songs of Solomon, Ruth, Ecclesiastes, Esther and Daniel.

THE ARTICLES OF MAIMONIDES

The articles of Maimonides also list laws similar to Talmud laws. "Maimonides produced just such a work although it was widely criticized when first seen, because he deleted so many references."[37]

MAIMONIDES 13 ARTICLES OF FAITH

1	The existence of the creator
2	His unity
3	His in-corporeality (God is Spirit, not matter)
4	His eternity
5	The obligation to serve and worship Him alone
6	The existence of prophecy
7	The superiority of Moses to other prophets
8	The revelation of the commandments at Sinai
9	The unchanging nature of the law
10	The omniscience of God
11	Retribution in the world and the next
12	The coming of the Messiah
13	The resurrection of the dead

---

37. Ibid., p. 51.

KABALA

This is another largely medieval development in Judaism. It is mystical tradition handed down from a teacher to his pupil, which helped the student to find unity with God. Legend has it that God taught the Kabala to the angels who in turn enlightened Adam, so that he might find his way back to God. It was known to Noah, Abraham, and Moses- who instituted the 70 Elders. "The primary book of Kabala is the Sefer ba Zobar or book of Splendour written between 1280 and 1286 by Moses de Leon in Spain, the heart of anti-Maimonides country."[38] To achieve union with God, the book suggests elevation through a path-which is represented on the tree of life. The fruits of the tree, the Sephirot, of which there are ten, symbolize the attainment of knowledge. The base of the tree has seven fruits the main five being: sovereignty-kingship, beauty, loving-splendor, kindness and judgment (severity and foundation are the last two). They fall under the conscious emotions on the way to elevation. All compound with energy centered along the spine. The top three are: understanding, wisdom, and crown/ humility. Understanding and wisdom comprise the conscious intellect section and 'crown' indicates the final state of elevation known as above consciousness.

Kabala-ism extends beyond this outline explanation and takes years to master. It was popular between 1500 and 1800. Interest in it has since declined, although its impact on Jewish folklore was substantial. The Kabala was borrowed by western occultists to form part of ritual magical texts. De Leon believed that people did talk with God, but that the encounter took place, not literally but in a dream. Anyone who was mentally prepared could receive prophecies. His belief in the power of reason was balanced by his unshakable faith in Moses and God.

If the Bible is the cornerstone of Judaism then the Talmud is the central pillar, soaring up from the foundation and supporting the entire spiritual and intellectual edifice. No other work has had a comparable influence on the theory and practice of Jewish life says Rabbi Adin Stein-Sulz.[39]

---

38. Ibid., p.56.
39. Ibid., p.51.

JEWISH CELEBRATIONS

THE SABBATH

The Jewish Sabbath is more than just a day of rest. Beginning on Friday evening at sunset and ending on Saturday at night-fall, the Sabbath has three aspects, a day of rest, a day of holiness, and a day of gladness.

BAR MITZVAH

This is a renewal of the covenant between God and the Jewish people. It takes place on the Sabbath following the 13th birthday for a Jewish boy and marks the advent of his religious duty with a Bar Mitzvah. On this day he is called for the first time to read publicly from the Torah, and he becomes a full-fledged member of the congregation. Afterwards he wears the Tefillin a black leather box which contains strips of parchment on which is inscribed sections of the Pentateuch. They are worn on the arm and forehead during morning prayers.

WEDDINGS

The family's triumphal day is a wedding. The traditional service may include the usual formal questions and end with the breaking of a glass to recall the destruction of Jerusalem. Marriage is considered sacred, though divorce is permitted. Jewish tradition makes the husband very much the master, but woman is held in the utmost esteem as mother and keeper of the home. "Love thy wife as thyself and honor her more than thyself" says the Talmud. "Be careful not to cause woman to weep, for God counts her tears."[40]

PRAISE

When the Israelite community gathered for worship, the individual had ample opportunity to praise Yahweh, to confess his sin, to seek Yahweh's aid for his own specific situation, and to make his vows and offerings to the Deity. The piety of the Psalter clearly reflects the place of the individual in temple worship. The Psalter (Psalms) contains prayers, hymns, petitions, and laments

---

40. Henry Luce, Time Life Incorporated, p. 138.

actually uttered by the worshippers. 150 Psalms have been collected and arranged in a set of five books. "Israel's worship must have consisted of much magical practice, much polytheism, much syncretistic worship."[41]

HOLY DAYS

ROSH HASHANAH AND YOM KIPPUR

(The Jewish New Year in September or October)   (The Day of Atonement)

Together, they form a ten day period of repentance, soul searching and return to God. They are considered to be High Holidays of the faith. Rosh Hashanah is a holiday that takes place in Tishrei, the 7th month of the Jewish calendar, with Nisan being the first. It is celebrated for two days and is both joyous and introspective. Traditionally it is harbingered by the sounding of the Shofar or ram's horn at the end of the morning service. It is linked to Yom Hadin. Yom Hadin means the Day of Judgment. On this day God opens the books of life and death which he then seals on Yom Kippur. At this time God decides the fate of all of Israel as a community and as individuals either in the book of life or death.

Historically for Yom Kippur (Yom Kippurim) lots were cast by the High Priest to select two goats (casting of lots is known as Pur). One was sacrificed before God on the altar in a purification ritual and on the other (called the Azazel) the sins of Israel were confessed. The Azazel was released to wander the desert so that it could carry the sins of the people away. Yom Kipper requires a strict 24 hours fast, a thorough weighing of one's past deeds, and synagogue prayer for God's mercy.[42]

PASSOVER

Next in importance among the holidays is Passover which occurs in March or April. It is a festival for recalling liberation from Egyptian bondage.

---

41. Karen Harrington, p. 428.
42. http://myjewishlearning.com/holidays, retrieved 7/16/12.

PURIM

March or April is a time for masquerades in which children re-enact Queen Esther's rescue of the Jews from the machinations of the tyrant Haman. Haman had cast lots to determine when to plot the Jews demise.

SHABUOT

The Feast of the Lord's Fruits (May or June) commemorates the handing down of the Ten Commandments and among reform families is the time for confirming boys and girls of 15 years of age.

SUCCOTH

An eight day Autumn Thanksgiving festival marks not only the gathering of the harvest, but the coming of the rains. It demands the building of leafy boughs which recall the flimsy shelters the Jews had after the flight from Egypt. The children recruit all their neighborhood friends- Catholic, Protestant and Jewish to aid in the project.

SIMCHATH TORCH

This celebration is given for rejoicing in the laws (September or October) and marks the end of the yearly cycle of Torah reading.

HANUKKAH

This is the Feast of Lights (November or December) and celebrates the victory of Judas Maccabaeus over the Syrians and the rekindling of the temple light. It also demonstrates the remarkable adaptability of Judaism and the inter relationship of family and faith. "Up to fifty years ago Hanukkah was a relatively unimportant festival, but it falls close to Christmas, and so Jewish families especially in the reform movement have come to emphasize the time for the children's sake. Mothers lead their young ones in hymn singing, cheer on the youthful top spinners in a special Hanukkah game (in which the top, referring to the temple light rekindling bears Hebrew initials of the words 'A mighty miracle occurred there'). They have a moving ceremony of the lighting of the Hanukkah menorah or candelabra, and many families provide gifts for the children on each day of the festival's eight nights."[43]

THE SYNAGOGUE

For years, the center of Jewish religious life had been the Temple in Jerusalem. When this was destroyed in 587 B.C., and the Jewish people departed to Babylon, they were deprived of an important religious focus. The prophet Jeremiah, still imprisoned in the ruins of Jerusalem urged his people by letter on God's behalf to seek the welfare of the city. He said in the book of Jeremiah "Where I sent you into exile and pray to God on its behalf for in its welfare you will find your welfare."

The original meaning of synagogue was 'a gathering'. It was probably drawn from the Greek word "Synagogen" to gather together. The synagogues became familiar features of every village and town. They were not to be farther apart than 1 mile in order to facilitate worship and the keeping of the commandment pertaining to the Sabbath. The gospels reveal that in the time of Jesus, there were synagogues in everyday use. When the temple in Jerusalem was destroyed for a second time in A.D. 70 the vacuum was filled by the Synagogue. The Synagogue in the local community became in time, the temple of Yahweh for the dispersed Jewish community.[44]

The Synagogues became the center of the community and the center of Jewish culture. People were drawn together not for sacrifice or rites and rituals alone but for congregational prayer and instruction. Synagogues have always been much more than that. Another important function of the synagogue was education. Perhaps this was the primary function particularly for the study of the Torah. Synagogues also acted (in the past) as bakeries to provide unleavened bread for the Passover celebration, and even as hostels. It must be noted that Israelite life and faith was so great

---

43. Henry Luce, p. 138.
44. Harrelson, Walter., Interpreting the Old Testament, Holt, Reinhart and Winston Inc. 1964. p. 429.

that the community could survive the destruction of the temple in A.D. 66-70.

DIASPORA

In the 6th century B.C., Babylonian invaders laid waste to much of Jerusalem, Judah, and Israel. Jewish people were forcibly removed from the Promised Land to which Moses had led them. Generations came and went but the dream of Israel, Holy Land remained alive. A Jewish hero Judah Maccabee (Judas Maccabeus) and his brothers resurrected the aspirations of the Israelites when they led a successful revolt against Syrian rulers of Jerusalem. The temple, which had been desecrated, was restored to the Jewish faith once more, but the liberation was short lived. By 63 B.C., the Roman Empire swallowed up Israel in their inexorable spread. The Roman influence on the daily lives of the Jews in the Holy Land greatly affected their worship. An uprising in A.D. 70 was ruthlessly crushed- the penalty being the destruction of their second temple. Within 70 years, the Romans expelled the Jews from their homeland. The Jews then became a nation-less people. Some went to North Africa, to Morocco, to Spain, France and England. Others sought refuge in Constantinople, Italy and Germany.

In the 19th century the Jewish nationalist movement was formed and was formally launched at the First Zionist Conference in Basle in 1897. "For the first time in centuries the desire of the Jews for a national homeland was voiced in the international arena."[45]

In 1901 a Jewish national Fund was established to buy land in Palestine. Tel Aviv was founded in 1919 to house a booming Jewish population. After the Holocaust in which European Jewry was decimated during World War II, the Zionist dream became a reality. Israel was created in 1948 as a homeland and a safe haven for the world Jews. Its history has not been without incident. The troubles began with the unhappy Arabs (their cousins) to reach a peaceful and happy settlement. The struggle has intensified and today there is constant warfare between the Jews and Arabs. This

---

45. Karen Harrington., p. 49.

35

centers around who has the right to nationhood.

AWAITING A SAVIOR

Jeremiah declared that the covenant made between God and Abraham had been broken. The prophets looked beyond the disaster to see a time when God would intervene to repair the damage. Others pinned their hopes on a Messiah that would come and vindicate his people.

Chapter 5

HINDUISM

Hinduism is a faith of one God or 330 million gods. There is no indisputable truth for Hindus, but many different aspects of the same truth.[46] This maze of mythology, mysticism, and free flowing belief has evolved over thousands of years. Charioteer riding Aryans overran India more than 3000 years ago and then superimposed their beliefs upon the indigenous religion of the country. The five main principles of Hinduism may be summed up as Parmeshivar (God) Prarthana (Prayer) Punerjanma (Rebirth) Punushartha (Law of Action) and Prani Daya (Compassion for Living Things).

Short on dogma and doctrine it is consequently unwieldy, eccentric, chaotic and difficult to understand. Hindus have enormous freedom in choosing which path to follow, "Perhaps the biggest influence on their faith is exerted by the Gurus. These are personal teachers who are less bothered with academia and more concerned with social and spiritual enlightenment. For years it was judged to be of greater value to hear words from the mouth of a Guru and learn by heart to repeat them in the next generation, than to sit down and simply read a book."[47]

Hindu teaching is centered in the Upanishads. It comprises 'Upa' - meaning near, 'Ni' - meaning down and 'shad' - meaning sitting. They are the collected wisdom of numerous Gurus, gathered by their pupils in Sanskrit between 500 and 200 B.C. The aim is to link the student to God by first illustrating the relationship or union that exists between man and God. It consolidated the view that there is only one God. Their predecessor, the Vedas, is the oldest of the Hindu scriptures. "This was the literature handed down by the Aryan invaders who swarmed over India from the North about 1750 B.C."[48]

It seems as if both Aryans and Israelites had similar quests for God. So we find mention of the story of Exodus under Moses,

---

46. Ibid., p. 62.
47. Ibid., p. 66.
48. Ibid., p. 67.

which took place around the same historical time as Aryan stories.

THE FOUR VEDAS

There are four Vedas, the most eminent being the first- the Rig Veda (Book of Mantra) or Veda of Praise. The rest include the Sama Veda (Book of Song), the Yajur Veda (Book of Ritual) , and the Atharva Veda (Book of Spell). The Sama Veda is a collection of melodies that are purely liturgical in nature. It puts many of the concepts of the Rig Veda into song. The Yajur Veda is used by priests as a guide for prayer and sacrificial ceremonies and bears remarkable similarity to the Egyptian book of the dead. The final Veda is often not considered as part of the Vedas by any scholars because of its simplicity in language in comparison to the others as well as its construction. The hymns are more eclectic in nature and refer mainly to spells and charms used in the Rig-Vedic society.[49a,b,]

In the Rig Veda there are 1,017 hymns divided into ten sections or Mandalas dedicated to the gods of the Aryans. Among the gods are Varuna, ruler of the heavens and seas and Indra, the warrior. The finale is the song of creation which suggests that there is an all powerful entity about which the gods knew nothing. The Rig Veda hymns is the collective work of many 'Rishis' or seers and tells in detail many of the different aspects of the Rig-Vedic civilization.[49c]

THE EPIC POEMS (PARANAS)

The Epic Poems or Mahabharata and Ramayana are collections of writing known as Paranas. The Mahabharata consists of 100,000 couplets which examine the feud between the Pandavas and the Kauravas with allegory. This mammoth work contains the Bhagavad Gita - the song of the "Adorable One" perhaps the best loved Hindu Scripture. One of the Pandavas, Arjun is filled with doubt before going into battle against the Kauravas who are after

---

49a.http://www.Hinduism.about.com/cs/vedasvedanta/a/aa120103a_htm retrieved 5/14/2011.
49b.Op.cit. p. 67.
49c.http://www.Hinduism.about.com/cs/vedasvedanta/a/aa120103a_htm retrieved 5/14/2011.

all Kinsmen. "His charioteer is the god Krishna in disguise who imparts his teachings, banishes Arjun's doubt, and impounds the necessity for devotion to God."[50] The masses of Hindus pay homage to many gods or worship just one of them as a personal god. This is fundamentally a matter of no real theological import since Hindu religious thought is dominated by the concept of monism – the oneness of all things, of gods as well as all living things."Though the complexity of the philosophy can be staggering to the western mind, Hindus feel the essentials can be clearly stated this way. To them all is Braham, including our own selves. Only through ignorance and deception do we see life as multiplicity instead of oneness, and our salvation consists in dispelling the illusion of 'I' and 'thou' and realizing that we, and all the world are part of the divine one."[51]

LOVE OF ALL

Even the lowest creatures are sacred. Seeing God in everything is a part of the Hindu. The Hindu's have a reverence for everything: trees and rivers, cows and ants. This reverence is expressed in one form as Ashima, or non violence to animals as well as humans and as a result most pious Hindus are vegetarians. The Hindu affection for the cow is something special, probably because throughout their history Indians have depended so heavily on the cow for pulling plows and carts and for milk and for fuel. Dried dung is still India's principal domestic fuel. For a Hindu to consume beef is a sacrilege - tantamount to cannibalism. All that kill cows the scripture warns "rot in hell for as many years as there are hairs on the body of the (slain) cow". Some Hindus bow respectfully to all cows that they pass, and wealthy men endow hostels to take care of old and decrepit cows.[52]

YOGA

This is ascetic discipline and the path to union with God. The really religious Hindu "pants after God as a miser after gold". His one burning desire is withdrawal from the world and single minded preoccupation with Brahma. Nowhere else in the world is

---

50. Op.cit. p. 67.
51. Luce,Henry. Editor in Chief. Time Life Incorporated, New York, 1959 p. 15.
52. Ibid., p. 23.

asceticism considered a national ideal, as it is in India. Its lure is so strong that even the small children sometimes run away from home to become Sudhus and become part of the group of people who have renounced the world. Yoga is the yoking of the mind to God. "One who practices Yoga is a Yogi. Yogis deny their appetites and some are said to have such control over their bodies that they can stop their heart beats for as much as one minute and hold their breath for hours."[53]

Most of India's revered heroes have been ascetics, but the ideal is so exalted that even a hero like Gandhi was not considered by the orthodox a real "holy man" because he involved himself with Indian nationalism and therefore worldly affairs. In the highest state, when the meditating yogi has cut off all sense perceptions, he is beyond family, caste, country, religious devotions, good and evil, time and space and even beyond himself because he is one with God.

DEATH

The biggest event in the life of the Hindu is really his death. When a Hindu thinks he is about to die, his first thought is to travel if possible to the holy city of Benares, where, by bathing in the sacred Ganges, he can become free from his sins. Benares has thus become a vast, bustling city of death. It teems with old and sick people, widows and cremation pyres in the Ghats on waterfront. Ghat stairways blaze day and night as a steady stream of corpses is brought there to be burned. For Hindus who regard Benares as the end of a tiresome journey, the atmosphere is almost that of a holiday.

By Hindu custom bodies of ordinary mortals must be burned. Only the holiest of holy men, the Sannyasis who have theoretically been united with Brahman, need not be burned. When a Sannyasi dies, his body is garlanded by his disciples and tenderly carried down to the Ghats where it is weighted with stones, reverently saluted then dropped into the river. As the body slowly sinks the disciples blow the conch shell and chant hymns, marking the joyous occasion of a human soul's re-entry into union with God."[54]

---

53. Ibid. p. 26.
54. Ibid. p. 29.

THE LAWS OF MANU

These laws are the comprehensive rules for spiritual, moral, ethical and civil dilemmas. It was the wisdom of the gods imparted to Manu that established the caste system and condemned countless thousands of people to misery over the ensuing centuries.

Hindus believe that some of the writing revered in their faith are Srati, (revelations of God), others are Smrti, (remembered text) which are not highly regarded.

THE VEDIC PRAYERS

In Hinduism, god is often represented by the sound of Om or Aum. The A stands for the power of God the creator, the U stands for God, the preserver, and the M for God the power to destroy. Hindus meditate to the sound of AUM. There are many popular Mantras chanted in Hinduism. Many of them are housed in The Rig Veda. Cited below are two prayers that are said regularly in contemporary Hinduism:

असतो मा सद्गमय ।

तमसो मा ज्योतिर्गमय ।।

मृत्योर्मामृतं गमय ।

ॐ शांति: शांति: शांति:

Asato maa sad-gamaya

Tamaso maa jyotir-gamaya

Mrityor-maa-mritan gamaya

Om shaantiḥ shaantiḥ shaantiḥ

Lead us from Untruth to Truth, from Darkness to Light, from Death to Immortality. Om peace, peace, peace.

सर्वे भवन्तु सुखिनः। सर्वे सन्तु निरामयाः।

सर्वे भद्राणि पश्यन्तु। मा कश्चित् दुःख भाग्भवेत्॥

Sarve bhavantu sukhinah sarve santu nirAmayAh sarve bhadrANi pashyantu mA kaScit dukha bhAg-bhavet

Let all be happy. Let all be free from disease. Let all see the Truth. May no one experience suffering. This has been translated elsewhere as follows, "Let there be good to all, let all be free of sickness, let all see good and, let none suffer." It is a mantra that is often used to open the Guyatri Mantra.

The Guyatri Mantra is a prayer from the Rig Veda that is considered to be a signature prayer. It has been chanted daily by generations of Hindus and reads:

Om Bhur Bhuva Svah

Tat Savitur Varenyam

Bhargo Devasya Dhimahi

Dhiyo Yo Naha Prachodayat

On the absolute reality and its planes,

On that finest spiritual light,

We meditate, as remover of obstacles

That it may inspire and enlighten us.

As it is sung, even the rhythmic cadence of the sound is thought to be imbued with spiritual significance.[55]

---

55. http://www.ganesh.us/mantara/mantra.html
http://www.shaivam.org/index.html
http://en.wikipedia.org/wiki/Prayer_in_Hinduism.,retrieved 9/26/2012

REINCARNATION

Concerns about death and the afterlife are probably what drives most people into the arms of a faith. "For Hindus the journey to unity with God is longer than most."[56] Hindus believe in reincarnation. That means the soul is reborn into another body after death to endure a further life. This is not a matter to rejoice over for the aim is to leave the wheel of rebirth, Samsana and to be reunited with Brahman, the Absolute.

The law of cause and effect governing reincarnation is called "karma" which translates from Sanskrit to "deed". In essence every physical action, word and every thought in this life is accounted for not only in this life but in the next. Goodness will be rewarded, while punishments await those who have erred. It is a chain, which cannot be broken but will hopefully come to a natural end if a person follows the three pure Precepts. These are cease evil, do good, and keep a pure mind.

In biblical terms, it adds up to the old adage of reaping what you sow. In Christian philosophy the results are seen as the days of reckoning, rather than in a new life or cycle of new lives. Hinduism provides more than just a faith. It is also a code for everyday living which encourages good conduct. Those people who are particularly evil may return to earth in the guise of an animal on another lower life form.

Karma is divided into 3 parts; 1) Agami - karma which refers to present causes and effects, 2) Prarabdha -karma which is already caused and is in a process of being effected 3) Sanchita - karma is similarly caused but has yet to take effect.

The belief in reincarnation dates back to the Vedas and is reinforced in the Upanishads. Like the Caste System, it has been used by priests as a stick to keep the lower in order in their place. Karen Harrington in History of Religion observes that "those claiming to be reincarnations of others might be able to recall names, dates and personal facts, they might recognize places and people unknown to them. They sometimes behave like the person they claim they once were, and finally they might look similar or

---

56. Karen Harrington. p. 68.

bear certain mirror image marks, sometimes birth marks have been associated with death wounds from a previous existence too."[57]

POSITIONS IN LIFE   The Caste System

India is famous for its Caste system,- ancient divisions of society into which people are born and may never leave. The Hindu Caste system or Varina began with four main divisions:

1 - Brahmin - the Priests
2 - Ksatrijas - the Warriors
3 – Vaisyas - the Merchants
4 - Sudras - the Servants (the untouchables).

According to mythology the Castes came from Parusha the father figure of mankind. The caste system was abolished in India in 1948 and discrimination was outlawed, thanks to Mahatma Gandhi who re-named the Sudras the Harijan or children of God.

HINDU TEMPLES

Hindus can engage in prayer or puja anywhere and everywhere. For them the universe is a temple of worship and most homes have a shrine at which puja is usually preformed three times daily. However "Hinduism is known for its exotic temples bedecked with flowers and fragrant with the smell of incense."[58] Many Hindus visit temples to pay homage to the Deity and pray. Although there is variety in age and shape, temples share some commonalities. These are:

- 1. A *statue* which acts as a temple guardian. When the temple is dedicated to Shiva the guardian is the bull Nandi. Vishnu's temple has the bird Garuda, and Dunga's a fierce Lion.
- 2. *Mandapa* which is a grand pillared hall beyond which lies the shrine. The object in the shrine represents the Deity and is covered by a canopy, or pyramid roof. Worship is directed less at the idol than at the spirit behind it. Hindu teaching decrees "one needs images and symbols as long as God is not realized in his true

---

57. Ibid. p. 69.
58. Ibid. p. 72.

form. It is God himself who has provided these various forms of worship to suit different stages of spiritual growth"[59]

- 3. These other images are the revered **Mohandas**, Gandhi, the Sikh founder Guru Narak and even Jesus who is honored as the great teacher of God's message.

PURIFICATION

Before approaching God the worshipper must be pure. A ritual daubing of the ears, nose, eyes, mouth, arms, body and legs with water achieves this. The priest then recites from the Vedas and prays to the chief gods.

CEREMONIAL OFFERING

This is an offering of love, art, and devotion open to everyone. A tray with five artistically designed lights is waved in front of the Deity and presented with flowers, incense, water and ether. All the foreheads in the temple whether they be human or image, are dotted with red paste before the congregation donates money. They then receive God's blessing by placing their hands over the flames and rubbing the heat into their forehead and hair.

HYMNS

Hymn singing is accompanied by tambourines, drums and communal clapping.

DANCING

"Dancing is another form of Hindu devotion and with the rise in popularity of ethnic dancing in the West, one of the most easily accessible to the westerner."[60]

HINDU CELEBRATIONS

THE FESTIVAL OF LIGHT (Diwali)

The tale of Diwali's victory by Krishna over the demon

---

59. Ibid. p. 72.
60. Ibid. p. 73.

Nanaka of Assam states that the vanquished Nanaka made one final request of Krishna "on the anniversary of my death everyone should be happy, wear new clothes, let off fireworks, burn lights to brighten the night, and send one another greetings."[61] Hindus who have moved from India to western countries often describe the season as "our Christmas". Another famous triumph; that of Vishnu over king Bali, is also given as the reason for celebrating Diwali.

HOLI (Pagwa or Holaka)

Holi is celebrated in spring. Originally an agricultural festival, it signifies the beginning of spring, and takes place on the day after the full moon in the Hindu month of Phalguna (early March). But it is the least religious holiday in Hinduism. During that time nature and people, throw off the gloom of winter and attend a public bonfire (the burning of Holika). They spray each other with colored powders and water and generally get a little wild.

Several myths are associated with the burning of Holika. In one Holika, who possessed magical powers, is alleged to have picked up her brother Prahlada and walked through a furnace in order to save him from his father Hiranyakasipy's wrath. His father had forbidden him to worship Vishnu but he persisted so he was to be punished. When she entered the flame with her brother, her powers were diminished. Holika died while Prahlada, who spent his time reciting the names of the gods emerged unscathed.[62] Some versions claim he ordered her to do so, and others say she was an evil aunt who begged him forgiveness upon her demise which is why her memory is commemorated.

THE GANGES

Ritual morning bathing is important to Hindus, as it leaves the body refreshed and ready for prayer. One way to achieve this is to dip in the river Ganges. The Ganges is so sacred that it is cited in prayers. One Hindu prayer lists 108 different names of the river. Hindu mythology claims that the Ganges was once the Milky Way.

---

61. Ibid.p.75.
62. http://www.religionfacts.com/hinduism/holidays/holi Retrieved 7/9/2011.

HINDU WORSHIP AROUND THE GLOBE

Outside of India, Hindu temples have become a focus for the community: Congregational prayer has assumed a greater importance and become more organized. There are no set times for worship. Hindus will adapt to the country in which they live. They will have a Sunday morning service in Britain or America. The worship is centered on the sacred fire (Havan), sparked in a profitable fire altar containing wood and clarified butter. Only the priest can initiate the offering of fire or Havan.

Chapter 6

ISLAM

Islam is a relative newcomer as a world religion in terms of its age. Islam however, is one of the success stories of the world's religions. It began in a dusty corner of Arabia fourteen centuries ago; which makes it the most modern of the great faiths. It came about through the efforts of one man, Mohammad. He broadcast the divine messages he received from God to all those who would listen. At first, only a few listened. Then as his audience grew, in the best tradition of prophets, he was driven out of his home town and ridiculed. His persistence and profound faith were ultimately rewarded when his band of followers multiplied and he turned the pagan face of Mecca toward God. "Today, there are millions of Muslims". The religion is dominant in the countries of North Africa, the Middle east, Western Asia, and Indonesia."[63]

Muslims pray to the God Allah. Allah in Arabic term comprising two words Al which means "The" and Illah which means "God". To Muslims the name Allah is preferable to that of God because it appears in the holy book the Quran. It has no male or female gender, and cannot be pluralized in the same way that "God" can become "gods". Harrington observed that the change of name from God is just one of the many ways in which Islam is widely misunderstood in the West. She attributed that a kernel of mistrust was planted centuries ago by the crusaders; and after the cruel violence between Muslims and Christians, the tolerance preached by both Mohammad and Christ was never credibly regained.

Mohammad was born about 570 A.D. in Mecca. Mecca was an important site. Its chief attraction was the Kaaba, a monument originally built by Abraham, "By the time of Mohammad's birth, the Kaaba was devoted to numerous Deities and was strewn with idols."[64]

Mohammad's father Abdullah died before he was born. His

---

63. Ibid. p. 112.
64. Ibid. p. 135.

mother died when he was six orphaning him. Care of the child passed to his blood grandfather who died just 2 years later. He became the ward of an uncle, and under his guardianship Mohammad forged a career in trade.

Mohammad had no formal education. He encountered the Christian, Jewish and pagan faiths, which prevailed among the travelers he met. He married Khadija a woman some 15 years his senior. She bore him some six or seven children, but his three sons died in infancy. At the age of 40, on Mt. Hira, the angel Gabriel appeared to him while he slept. Mohammad regarded this experience as the "Night of Power" or "Night of Destiny". He had regular revelations, which were later to become assembled as the Qur'an or Koran.

Mohammad would fall into a trance, the onset of which he could not control. As the intensity of the trance subsided he would recite verses in a style completely alien to his own. Mohammad preached his own religion urging the Meccans to reject idolatry and worship only one God. He soon discovered that his enthusiasm was not shared by his fellow Meccans. He and his faithful few, fled to Yathrib in 622 A.D. which later became year 1 of the Muslim calendar.

From Yathrib he consolidated his position and united his army of 300 in preparation for conflict. His campaign gained momentum until 630 A.D. when he marched victoriously into Mecca. "His first act was to smash the images of pagan gods which decorated the Kaaba, leaving just one picture of Jesus and Mary untouched."[65]

Mohammad urged the people to turn to God. He returned to Yathrib (Medina) the city of the prophet, and to his family. After this Khadijah died, and Mohammad, took other wives. There were ten in total and two Concubines, although his dream of having a son was never fulfilled.

Despite a natural tolerance of other religions, Mohammad felt bound to expel or exterminate the colonies of Jews, who

---

65. Ibid. p. 135.

vehemently denied his message. Mohammad died of intestinal problems in 632 A.D.

THE QUR'AN

Centuries after the death of Mohammad, his words continue to echo in the ears of every Muslim. The Qur'an says to its followers that it is God's last word spoken to their prophet Mohammad. The revelations that eventually comprised the Qur'an were taken from a heavenly book containing God's wisdom. All of the Holy Books containing the gospel of Jesus and the Jewish Torah were taken from the divine charter called the mother of the books. God decided to impart still more, so that the Arabs would be addressed in their own language. The Qur'an contains 6666 verses written in Arabic, recorded as how Mohammad wanted it to be remembered.

TEACHINGS OF THE QUR'AN

The five pillars of Islam

1. SHAHABAD – is the principal pillar of Islam and centers on of the confession of faith. There is only one God and Mohammad is his final prophet. The relevant lines of the Qur'an which affirm this belief are repeated at the start and end of the daily prayers performed five times a day and again during periods of meditation. It is a daily reminder that a belief in false gods is one of the cardinal sins in Islam.

2. SALAT - Prayers should be said five times every day. This gives every Muslim a guaranteed time of tranquility to reflect on the faith. Prayer is said with the face turned toward Mecca. When a Muslim bows down facing Mecca he does so in the knowledge that millions are doing just the same, around the globe and that repetition is supremely comforting.

3. ZAKAT - (Almsgiving) This practice helps to link all members of the Community, for as Mohammad puts it, if one suffers, then all others rally in response. Its aims are mutually beneficial. The giver is purged of selfishness and atones for sins, while the recipient vanquishes the powerful emotion of envy. The prophet did not expect his people to impoverish themselves, but to give proportionately of their wealth.

4. SAWM - is a month long daytime fast. Sawm is not just for the ascetically minded. Every adult, male or female is expected to undertake the fast. Only the unwell, mentally ill, children under twelve, pregnant, travelling or menstruating may be exempt. It is an act of union with God. During the calendar month of Ramadan, Muslims are obligated to feed a needy person for every day missed on fast as soon as possible afterwards.

Sawm has been a feature of Muslim life since 623 A. D. which is year 2 of the Muslim calendar. At that time Mohammad called for a 24 hour fast to mark the anniversary of the flight from Mecca to Medina.

5. HAJJ - or pilgrimage to Mecca which Muslims are urged to make at least once in a lifetime. The trek is made during the Islamic month of Dhail Hajj'i. The word Hajj means visits to the revered place to pay homage. This visit is not only to honor Mohammad but also Abraham. In Islamic philosophy he was one of the earliest in a line of God's prophets on earth which ended with Mohammad.

"The legend associated with Mecca extends to the very beginning of Biblical times. It's said that Adam expelled from paradise came to the site of the city to build a temple in praise to God. Using stones from Mt. Sinai, the Mount of Olives and Mount Lebanon, Adam created the first Kaaba and encrusted it with gems. Unfortunately its fate was not a happy one. It was covered by flood waters at the time of Noah and its finery reduced to the nondescript by the time the region again became a desert.

Abraham came here with his maid servant Hagar and their son Ishmael. He abandoned them to the will of God. Hagar made desperate attempts to seek water, running between Mount Marwa and the hill of Safu, seven times. Finally, she saw an angel who asked her why she was weeping, "I thirst" she sobbed. At that the angel rushed to the ground with a wing up, and up bubbled a fresh spring that was christened Zamzam.

Hagar and Ishmael prospered at the site and finally Abraham returned to rebuild the Kaaba on the site of Adam's original monument. In it he incorporated a sacred stone. It is reputed to have been the heavenly symbol of man's soul and was luminous

51

white. The stone was eventually blackened by man's sins. The Kaaba is a striking black box, not a building and remains key to the complex ritual of Hajj."[66] It exists today, having since been identified as a piece of meteorite.

The official opening of the Hajji takes place in the seventh day of the month. A day later the pilgrims make their way to the village of Mina five miles away. At sunrise on day nine they go to Arafat for a sermon, which lasts for much of the afternoon. The next assembly point is the valley of Muzdalifa. The aim is to arrive there in time for evening prayers. Here they gather stones for the ceremony at Mina. The following day, a pillar representing the devil is showered with pebbles. "Two million people may be taking part, each launching seven rocks. Few of the stones reach their intended target and most of them fall on the heads and bodies of fellow pilgrims."[67]

There follows a feast sacrifice. The pilgrims then shave, wash, and cut their hair and return to Mecca to circle the Kaaba seven times. Their aim is to touch the black stone, but most must be content to salute it from afar.

MOSQUES

A Mosque is usually thought to be equivalent of a Christian church - that is, the venue for worship. To the Muslim the whole world is a Mosque, a suitable place for prayer. Prayers can be carried out in company or alone. All that is needed is a small area of clean ground, which is why a prayer mat is needed. Muslims pray 5 times a day, at dawn, midday, late afternoon, evening, and last thing at night. It would be impossible to perform all of their devotions in the confines of one particular building. The Mosque remains central to the life of a Muslim community as somewhere to study the Qur'an and for communal prayer. The great mosque at Mecca is the most sacred, but the Blue Mosque in Istanbul is probably the most familiar in the west.

---

66. Ibid. p. 142.
67. Ibid. p. 143.

THE TRIUMPH OF ISLAM

The momentum of conquest carried the Arabs eastward to India, westward to the Atlantic and across the strait of Gibraltar into Spain, Portugal and France. In 732, in one of the decisive battles of history, the Muslims were halted by the Franks near Tours. "Yet their energies were not yet spent. The Ninth, tenth and Eleventh centuries were the golden age of Islam. Awakened by exposure to the Greco-Roman, Byzantine and Persian heritage, Islam evolved a brilliant culture of its own. Art, Philosophy and Poetry flourished in Baghdad and other great cities of the Arab Empire. Mathematics and medicine advanced. Muslim architects created master works like Córdoba's Mosque."[68] The message of Islam continued to spread, born by merchants and wandering Sufi's (mystics) across Asia to Indonesian Islands.

RAMADAN

Ramadan is the month of fasting when the devil is put in chains. It is a time when the gates of paradise are open, the gates of hell shut and the devil is enchained. It is a time of fasting. Mohammad ordained an entire month of fast days but limited fasting to the day light hours "eat and drink until so much of the dawn appears that a white thread may be distinguished from a black then keep the fast completely all night."[69]

The fast of Ramadan is the most scrupulously observed by many Muslims of all religious duties. Excepting only the sick and aged, young children and pregnant women, all believers must refrain between dawn and dark, from taking food or drink and from any sexual act. A day's fast can be vitiated by a single lie or glance of passion. All trade and public affairs slow down during the day, but once the sunset cannon sounds, life begins anew.

When Ramadan has passed the little Bairam begins. A festival somewhat analogues to Christmas time marked by grateful prayers, expansive good will and the giving of presents.

---

68. Op. Cit. pg 102.
69. Henry Luce pg. 114.

SECTS OF ISLAM

1 - The Shiites

The Shiites share all the basic beliefs of orthodox Islam, and derive from those who differed over the choice of Caliph (successor) the ruler of all Muslims. The Shiites form the largest group of Muslims. Hussein, Mohammad's grandson's death brought about the sect's establishment. His dying in battle is linked to him atoning for man's sins, an idea that is novel to Islam.

The Shiites live mainly in Iran and Iraq, Yemen and the Indian subcontinent are themselves divided into other subgroups. The largest subgroup, the Twelvers, are recognized as legitimate twelve Imams.

2 - The Sunnis

They comprise about 90% of the world's Muslims. The Sunnis (orthodox) group has always held that the post of Caliph or successor as the ruler of all Muslims is elective, but restricted to members of the Koreish - the tribe of Mohammad. This contrasts to the Shiites who contend that the post is God-given though open to descendants of Mohammed's family through his son-in-law Ali. They view their leaders (Imams) as human while the Shiites view their leaders as infallible manifestations of God who can interpret the Qur'an perfectly. Their leaders are known as Mujtahads. The Sunnis have no sects but respect four major schools of Muslim Law and are dispersed throughout all Muslim countries.[70]

THE CALL TO PRAYER

A local crier or Muezzin calls from the top of towers or Minarets at the dawn of each day. "God is most great, I bear witness that there is no God but God. I bear witness that Mohammad is the messenger of God. Come to prayer. Prayer is better than sleep"[71] His chants will ring out throughout the streets and houses an additional four times during the day.

70.http://www.religionfacts.com/islam/comparison_charts/islamic_sects.htm retrieved 12/22/13.
71. Karen Harrington., pg 145.

WORSHIP WITHIN THE MOSQUE

The word mosque means "place of prostration". At least once a day the ritual of prayer begins with thorough washing of hands, face, head, legs and feet. At the Mosque, a fountain or Fauwara is provided at its perimeter. With bare feet, the worshipper enters the prayer hall or Zulla beneath the dome. Floors and ceilings might well be covered with intricate patterned tiles, the decorations often ornately drawn out words or letters in the Qur'an.

There is little else to catch the eye. Pictures and statutes are forbidden as being images, which may distract from the worship of God. There is no furniture apart from the reading desk or Mimbar. The floor is covered with mats, which are used for prayer, but there are no chairs. On the walls there is the Muhrab, a decorative niche which indicates the direction of Mecca. With their bodies facing Mecca and their souls before God, the worshippers pray, uttering verses from the Qur'an.

Away from the Zulla is a screened area reserved for women. It is still considered un-orthodox to have women praying alongside men at the mosque. Integration between men and woman is accelerated in some countries. Adult males traditionally gather at the mosque on Fridays to hear a sermon from the Imam or religious leader. This is a tradition that was begun by Mohammad in Medina.

FUNDAMENTALISM

"The western media often give the impression that the embattled and occasionally violent form of religiosity known as "fundamentalism" is purely an Islamic phenomenon. This is not the case"[72] Fundamentalism is a global fact and has surfaced in every major faith in response to the problems of our modernity. There is Fundamentalist Judaism, Fundamentalist Christianity, Fundamentalist Hinduism, and Fundamentalist Buddhism. This type of faith surfaced first in the Christian world in the United States at the beginning of the twentieth century. This was not accidental. "Fundamentalism is not a monolithic movement.

---

72. Ibid., pg. 164.

Each form of fundamentalism even within the same tradition, develops independently, and has its own symbols and enthusiasms, but its different manifestations all bear a family resemblance."[73] Fundamentalist movements in all faith share certain characteristics. They reveal a deep disappointment and disenchantment with the modern experiment, which has not fulfilled all that it promised. They also express real fear. They are convinced that the secular establishment is determined to wipe religion out. Fundamentalism looks back to the "Golden Age" before the corruption of modernity, for inspiration. The fundamentalist community can be seen as the shadow side of modernity.

It can also highlight some of the darker sides of modern experiment. "Very often, fundamentalists begin by withdrawing from main stream culture to create an enclave of pure faith as for example within the ultra-orthodox Jewish community in Jerusalem or New York."[74]

Muslim fundamentalism began in the Sunni world with Sayyid Qutb (1906-66), who was greatly influenced by Abu'l A'la Mawdudi an Indian Theologian and Journalist. In 1953 he joined the Muslim brotherhood hoping to give western democracy an Islamic dimension that would avoid the excess of a wholly secularist ideology. In 1956 he was imprisoned by Al Nasser for membership in the Brotherhood. In concentration camp he became convinced that religious people and secularists could not live in peace in the same society. Qutb went further than Mawdubi who had seen the Muslim societies as Jubili. He applied the term Jubiliyyah which in conventional Muslim historiography had been used simply to describe the pre-Islamic period in Arabia. Qutb espoused a form of Islam that distorted both the message of the Qur'an and the prophet's life. He told Muslims to model themselves on Mohammad, separate themselves from mainstream society, (as Mohammad had made hijrah from Mecca to Medina) and then engage in a violent jihad. The same principle underlies the return to Islamic dress.

In 1930 Wallace Fard founded the Black Muslim group. He

---

73. Ibid., pg. 164.
74. Ibid., pg. 167.

was a peddler in Detroit. After his mysterious disappearance in 1934, Elijah Mohammad took over. He claimed that "God had been incarnated in Fard, that white people are inherently evil and that there was no life after death – all views that are heretical from an Islamic perspective."[75] The Nation of Islam demanded a separate state for African Americans to compensate them for the years of slavery, and is adamantly hostile to the west.

REACTION TO MUSLIM FUNDAMENTALISM

Today however there is much western hostility towards Islam. This springs from ignorance. There are many in the religio-political group in the United States who attribute the downing of the twin towers of the World Trade Center in New York, and the attack on the Pentagon on September 11th 2001 to the planning and orchestration of Muslim fundamentalists, and extend this belief to include all Muslims. Many Muslims have been ostracized, and jailed for this reason. It may be equally true to say that fundamentalists within the Christian religion have contributed to this suspicion, but let me hasten to say that Islam is not a "terrorist" religion. It is an unfair and unjust claim to link all Muslims and all fundamentalists with terrorism. A fanatical fringe may be "lunatic" but not a religion.

---

75. Ibid., pg. 177.

Chapter 7

BUDDHISIM

Buddhism is a religion of introspection. Meditation and concentration are key because the Buddhist takes an inner journey not to God but to bliss. Observers define Buddhism as a philosophy and not a religion. "Ironically, Buddhism was all but extinguished in its homeland of India, but became established in its various forms in Nepal, Tibet, Vietnam, China, Korea, Japan Sri Lanka, Burma, Thailand, Laos, and Kampuchea."[76]

Buddhism has attracted a following in the west; particularly among those who are disillusioned with the material world and seek an alternative. Some estimates put the number of Buddhists worldwide at 200 million. Others claim it is closer to one third of the population of the globe.

SIDDHARTHA (Buddha)

Buddha was born Siddhartha Gautama in about 563 B.C. to royal and wealthy parents of the Sakya clan, a Hindu warrior caste. Siddhartha lived in splendor in the town of Kapilavastu in the foothills of the Himalayas and grew up to become as accomplished scholar and student of martial arts. His mother Maya died a week after his birth, and he was brought up by his sister. She later became queen by marrying Siddhartha's father Śuddhodana. At age 16 Siddhartha married his cousin Yasodharā, a beautiful princess who bore him a son Rahula.

Siddhartha became troubled by the human conditions facing his people. When he was 29, he slipped away to sample life in the outside world. He encountered an old man, a sick man, a corpse being taken for cremation, and a shaven headed holy man. The first three exhibited signs of suffering, while the fourth was marked by inner peace and contentment. Siddhartha was deeply influenced by what he had seen and resolved to discover the cause and cure of such suffering. Under cover of darkness, he rode away from home on a horse, gave away his worldly belongings, shaved his head and

---

76. Karen Farrington, pg. 91.

adopted a life of an ascetic.

The Buddha's foot prints have long been venerated by his followers. "It is recounted that the king of Nago pleaded for Buddha to leave a token by which he might be remembered. The Buddha obliged by pressing his foot into the sandy shore of the Nammada River. Every year Buddhists remember the incident through the water festival of Songkran."

PHILOSOPHY OF BUDDHISM - The Four Noble Truths

- 1. Human life is full of suffering
- 2. People themselves create this suffering by trying to cling on to worldly pleasures. The emergence of this craving is called Samodaya.
- 3. If people set their feelings free and abandon material hopes and dreams, then suffering would end, creating a state of Nirvana.
- 4. The Eight Fold Path or Magga is the route by which people can liberate themselves from suffering.

THE EIGHT FOLD PATH

To help his disciples win passage to Nirvana, the Buddha established an eight-point charter for living, which would help his adherents put suffering behind them and achieve the necessary goodness and insight. The approach concentrated on morality, meditation and wisdom. The eight fold path is listed

1   Right views

2   Right thoughts

3   Right speech

4   Right actions

5   Right occupation

6   Right effort

---

77. Ibid., pg. 92.

7   Right mindedness

8   Right concentration

THE PATH TO NIRVANA

The Buddha urged his followers to have the "right views" that is to have a positive attitude about others as well as themselves. To achieve this entails a degree of faith in the words of the Buddha. With that comes the duty to consider the plight of others with sympathy and understanding and to back those "right thoughts" with "right speech" by never saying things that are hurtful or telling lies "The right action" is of course, good conduct earned by not killing or maiming and not stealing the possession of others. Good Buddhists will choose the right occupation, a job that does not involve cheating on others or causing injury to anyone or anything."[78] By following the eight fold path Buddhists are making the "right effort" and living as Buddha intended. Right mindfulness is being aware of the consequences of personal actions. Only by being aware can Buddhists halt a ripple effect, by which one action may affect other people. The "right concentration" is the tranquility which they should find in pursuing the Eight Fold Path.

THE FIVE PRECEPTS

The Buddha left a simple code which was named the Five Precepts. They reflect the nature of the Eight Fold Path but are not equivalent. They are:

1   Be compassionate to all living things and do not harm or kill other people or animals.

2   Do not steal or take what has not been given. Always be generous to those in need.

3   Avoid alcohol and drugs because they cloud the mind.

4   Do not tell lies or say bad things about others.

5   Respect others and abstain from sexual immorality

---

78. Ibid., pg. 96.

TWO VEHICLES OF BUDDHISM

There are three main branches of Buddhism: **Theravada** which is the oldest form and known as 'The way of the Elders and the Little Vehicle,' **Mahayana** is known as the Greater Vehicle, and the third is **Vajrayana** which is unique and led by the Dalai Lama. The first two factions are considered the main factions.

Mahayana Buddhism is the less severe interpretation of the Buddha's teaching and is known as the "Great Vehicle" because it is open to all to pursue while Theravada or the "Little Vehicle" is more rigid and reserved for those who wish to pursue monastic life. In simple terms, the movement split soon after the death of the Buddha with Theravada doctrine insisting that only monks could achieve Nirvana. "It remains the dominant form of Sri Lanka, Burma, Thailand, Laos and Kampuchea. Mahayana Buddhism opens the door to all and has achieved the majority of followers."[79]

There has been sporadic rivalry between the two major factions, but for the most part communities live contentedly side by side because tolerance is an important fact of Buddhism. The saffron monks with their shaven heads are common in both strains of Buddhism, as are the nuns or devout woman.

Bodhisattvas or people who are on the path to enlightenment are common to Mahayana Buddhism. This includes living persons who are on a Bodhisattva path or a celestial Bodhisattva (goddess or god) who has renounced final enlightenment in order to help other beings.

The most important deities include such beings as: (Sanskrit names used here) Tara, Manjushri or Manjusri, Avalokitesvara, Ksitigarbha, Samantabhadra, Maitreya. Tara in particular is very popular and is known as the Savior Goddess. She has two forms Green and White and is the principal deity of Tibet.[80] Gautama believed himself to be the Seventh Buddha and others were to follow in his footsteps. The Buddha's are not deities. They are the subject of devotion by monks, nuns and pilgrims.

---

79. Ibid., pg. 99.
80. http://www.religionfacts.com/buddhism/beings/bodhisattvas

As in other religions, Buddhism spread by word of mouth and the teachings of the Buddha were handed down from generation to generation. The holy book of Buddhism became known as the Pali Canon. It is so named because Pali is a variation of Sanskrit and is the language in which the text is recorded. There are three (Tripitaka or Tipitaka) sections or 'baskets' to these vast scriptures: the basket of discipline, the basket of special teachings, and the basket of Sutras.

NIRVANA

This is the state of complete bliss or state of nothingness to which the Buddhist aspire through the Eight Fold Path. "Nirvana is the 'noble truth of the stopping of suffering'. Because when it is reached there is renunciation, and so on, and there does not remain even one sensory pleasure, it is called renunciation, surrender, release. Nirvana is without a source, it is un-aging and undying. Because there is no source, no aging or dying it is permanent. Because it is attainable by means of the special cognition perfected by unfailing efforts, because it was spoken of by Buddha, because it has existence in the ultimate meaning, Nirvana is not non-existent."[81]

Unlike some other great religions Buddhism preaches a system of human conduct, primarily on rationality and relying very little on the supernatural. "In its history which stretches back 2500 years Buddhism has been one of the greatest civilizing forces the Far East has ever known, having stimulated the Arts, and contributed profound ideas to the great Tang Dynasty culture of China in the Seventh to the tenth centuries A.D. and brought civilization to Japan. Today, it is the dominant religion of Burma, Thailand, Tibet, Laos and Ceylon, and is a vast spiritual influence elsewhere in Asia."[82]

---

81. Ibid., p. 67.
82. Henry Luce. p. 39.

Chapter 8

CHRISTIANITY

The religion has grown from the extraordinary talents of one man, Jesus who lived over 2000 years ago, into the largest religion in the world today, with some 170 million followers. It is Jesus' death and his subsequent resurrection, symbolizing the triumph of good over evil, upon which Christianity is based. The central elements of Christian faith, unlike any others, is the suffering endured by the Messiah intertwined with mystic symbolism.

The story of Jesus' birth is fascinating. Mary and Joseph traveling to Bethlehem for a census and bedding down for the night in a stable where there was no room at the inn, brings a cozy glow to listeners. There are Shepherd's, lambs, wise men and angels to embellish the story. The synoptic gospels Matthew and Luke record the story. St Mark and St John omit the narrative. In John, Jesus is the incarnate word 'that became flesh and dwelt among us, full grace and truth.'

Jesus was born into a Jewish family. He attended the synagogue school and picked his disciples from the Jewish community. Under the Roman occupation the Jewish religious observances became lax. There were Pharisees who were strict and severe in their interpretation of the Jewish law, along with the equally ardent Hassidim (pious ones), the Sadducees, and the Essenes. All were in opposition of Roman ideals. Both Old Testament priests and the Zealots militant opposed the Romans, the Scribes, the Lawyers and the Rabbis (teachers).

Jesus became a rebel with a cause. At age 12 he slipped away from Joseph and Mary during a visit to Jerusalem for Passover, and was found day's later discussing religion with temple elders. Jesus was baptized in the Jordan River by John the Baptist. The Bible states a heavenly voice declared "Thou art my beloved son; in thee I am well pleased".

Jesus went into the desert to fast for 40 days and nights, resisting temptation by the devil before returning to start his ministry which lasted less than four years. Jesus taught that the way to salvation was through love of God and man. He emphasized the value of charity, humility, repentance and forgiveness, and kept the company of society's outcasts to prove his point. His miracles included restoring sight to the blind, speech to the dumb, and hearing to the deaf. He cured those suffering from leprosy, epilepsy, demonic possession and paralysis, and on three occasions he raised the dead. The pervasive words of Jesus' preaching and the miracles he performed galvanized the local population. He called into question the wisdom and merit of the existing religious hierarchy, and soon the religious leaders collaborated in order to rid themselves of this irritant.

Jesus was always sympathetic with man's plight as seen in his miracles and parables. He raised from the dead the son of a widow at Nain. So moved was Jesus by the weeping mother that he touched the funeral bier and said "young man I say to thee, arise." The twelve year old daughter of the synagogue elder Jairus was likewise restored to life. He raised his friend Lazarus after the latter had died for four days. He revealed a mastery over the forces of nature to sooth the anxieties of the disciples during stormy weather by walking upon water. This occurred after he had fed with just five loaves and two fishes, the 5000 people who came to listen to him preach in a desert. The remainder of the divine feast filled a dozen baskets.

A summary of his teachings is found in the Sermon on the Mount (a collection of sermons on His sayings).[83] Popular among these sayings are the *Beatitudes*. There are nine Beatitudes. Each begins with a blessing and ends with a reward.

1. Blessed are the poor in spirit for theirs is the kingdom of God.

2. Blessed are those who mourn for they shall be comforted.

3. Blessed are the meek, for they shall inherit the earth.

4. Blessed are those who hunger and thirst after righteousness for they shall be satisfied.

---

83. Holy Bible. Revised Standard Version. Matthew 5 – 7.

5. Blessed are the merciful, for they shall obtain mercy.

6. Blessed are the pure in heart, for they shall see God.

7. Blessed are the peacemakers, for they shall be called the children of God.

8. Blessed are those who are persecuted for righteousness sake for theirs is the Kingdom of God.

9. Blessed are you, when men shall revile you and persecute you and utter all kinds of evil against you falsely on my account. Rejoice, and be glad, for your reward is great in heaven for so men persecuted the prophets who were before you.

Another important aspect of his teaching is in the Model Prayer or Disciples Prayer, often referred to as the *Lord's Prayer*, found in Matthew 6:9-13. In these verses he taught the Disciples how to pray by first addressing God. The Lord's Prayer consists of eight sections:

1.   The fatherhood of God and the brotherhood of man.

2.   The nature of God who is infinite Holy omnipotent, omnipresent, omniscient. Philosophical theologian Paul Tillich refers to God as the Divine Absolute, the ground of being. Thomas Aquinas referred to God as the Un-caused, cause or the unmoved mover.

3.   The Kingdom of God or God's sovereign rule of the world. The Kingdom of God is similar to that which is in heaven. It is a Kingdom of love and peace. Jesus taught that the Kingdom of God is within you. It is not meat and drink. The Kingdom of God is translated into the Church. The Disciples are called to extend the Kingdom through the preaching of the gospel and teaching.

4.   The will of God. Christians are to pray that God's will be done on earth. The divine order will supersede all our longings and desires. What He wills, He will grant.

5.   God's providential love and sustenance. Give us this day our daily bread. This petition falls midway in the prayer. God is first; our needs are secondary. He supplies bread for the day. Our

daily needs are met.

6. Forgiveness of our sins. God forgives our sins even so we should forgive one another. If we confess our sins He is faithful and just and will forgive and cleanse us from all unrighteousness.[84]

7. Our forgiveness of one another. We must also forgive those who sin against us. Jesus taught "If we forgive men their trespasses your heavenly father will forgive you, but if you do not forgive their trespasses, neither will your father forgive your trespasses."[85]

At Cesearea Phillipi during Peter's great confession, "You are the Christ" Jesus empowered him with the ability to forgive "whatever sins you loose on earth will be loosed in heaven; whatever you bind on earth will be bound in heaven."[86]

8. His sustaining grace. Deliver us from evil. God does not lead us into temptation but He will protect us from the evil one. God protects, comforts, and shields in times of grave danger. Total dependence on Him is required. Then we will be delivered, and come to appropriate the goodness and marvels of his grace.

CHRIST THE SYMBOL OF FAITH

At the Passover feast of A.D, 29 or 30, Jesus and the twelve disciples gathered somberly while the rest of the city commemorated the Exodus of the Jews from Egypt. Jesus blessed and broke the bread and gave it to His disciples saying "Take, eat, this is my body. Then he passed around the red wine, declaring "This is my blood, shed for many for the remission of sins."[87] It is this act that became the foundation of Eucharist or Holy Communion. Some denominations refer to it as The Lord's Supper.

Jesus was arrested, following his betrayal by Judas. Sensing danger, his disciples ran off. Peter denied three times before dawn, that he was an associate of the arrested man.

---

84. Ibid., 1 John 1: 9-10.
85. Ibid., Matthew 6: 16-18.
86. Ibid., Matthew 16: 15-19.
87. Ibid., Matthew 26: 26-28.

THE CRUCIFICTION

Jesus was accused of blasphemy by the High priest, convicted and taken in chains to Pontius Pilate, the Roman Governor. Pilate would have released him, but the mob chose another condemned man Barabbas for the reprieve, and Jesus was crucified. Crucifixion was agonizing and reserved for the low criminals as a particularly demeaning way to die. Victims were flogged and forced to walk to the scene of their impending death, dragging the beam of the cross on which they would die. Death was mercilessly slow. A notice detailing the felon's name and crime was pinned at the top of the cross. In Jesus' case it apparently read INRI. - Jesus Nazarenous Rex Indaerum; Jesus of Nazareth, King of the Jews. With a crown of thorns on His head and a baying crowd, the humiliation of Jesus was complete. At noon that Friday darkness cloaked the land for three hours. Jesus cried out before His death "My God, MY GOD, why hath Thou forsaken me". At His last breath, the curtain in the temple was torn in two and the area struck by an earthquake.

THE RESURRECTION

The evening of the Crucifixion (Friday) the wealthy Joseph of Aramathea won permission to claim Jesus' body. He wrapped it in a shroud and put it in a tomb which was covered by a large bolder. Soldiers guarded the entrance, fearing the body would be snatched away by extremist followers. On Sunday, Mary Magdalene and other women disciples found the tomb empty and were told by an angel that Jesus had been raised. They were very doubtful and said that until they saw him with their own eyes they would not believe. That same day he appeared to two men as they journeyed toward Emmaus. The sight of him re-enforced their beliefs. For 40 days Jesus appeared to his faithful followers numbering as many as 500 before he ascended to God; the mortal man having become the immortal. Two natures, humanity and divinity, were vested in Him. Jesus taught that he was the resurrection and the life. He who believes in Him shall never die, but will enjoy continues felicity with him in the hereafter.

St. Paul, writing to the church at Corinth instructed them that Christ has been raised from the dead, the first fruits of those who had fallen asleep "For as by one man came death, by one man has come also the resurrection of the dead. For as in Adam all die so also in Christ shall all be made alive."[88]

THE DISCIPLES

When Jesus began his ministry he realized that the task of spreading the word of God was immense; so he recruited twelve disciples to assist. Significantly, the number of disciples mirrored the number of Jewish Tribes that entered Israel. The dozen together with Matthias (who replaced Judas Iscariot), and St Paul were later known along with other Christian missionaries as apostles and carried on his ministry. What most convinced them about Jesus was (1) his ability to perform miracles (2) his parables and teaching (3) his identification with the poor and outcasts (sinners) and (4) his resurrection from the dead (5) his gift of the Holy Spirit which he had promised them.

PENTECOST AND THE BIRTH OF THE CHURCH

Fifty days after the crucifixion, the disciples gathered in the upper room in Jerusalem in anticipation for the descent of the Holy Spirit. A divine fervor filled the room as the Holy Spirit descended on them. Accompanying it, came the gift of speaking in tongues, (languages) which endorsed their loyalty and commitment to Christ, and enabled them to communicate with the many races of the region.

The disciples all became missionaries and soon the gospel began to spread through "Jerusalem, Judea, Samaria, and on to the uttermost part of the earth, (Acts 1:8)." All the disciples suffered martyrdom on the basis of their faith in Christ and His Kingdom. Chief of which was Peter and the apostle John. Tradition asserts that Peter was crucified and John was exiled to the isle of Patmos where he was thrown in a boiling caldron of oil. It was on Patmos that John penned the Apocalypse (Revelation) envisaging the New Jerusalem coming down from God.

They all penned the gospels with St Peter and St Paul being responsible for the Epistles. Their writings, and the gospel, were based on the words and works of Jesus. These along with the

---

88. Ibid., 1 Corinthians 15: 20-25.

Epistles came to be known as the New Testament. The Church became a living reality on earth through the preaching and teaching of the Apostles. They were not daunted by persecution. They left their inscription on the Catacombs and the memorials erected in their honor throughout the Middle East or Holy land and around the world including the Vatican City with its Basilica of St. Peter; The Sistine Chapel; Cathedrals of St. Peter and St Paul in Rome and in London.

THE EARLY EXPRESSION OF CHRISTIANITY

At first, Christians were regarded as a Jewish Sect, and as such were left in peace. When Christians refused to worship the Roman gods they earned the enmity of the locals. Wild rumors circulated about their behavior, to include orgies, incest, and cannibalism. The latter accusation almost certainly grew out of the Eucharist in which the body of Christ the form of bread or a wafer is consumed. When Rome was burned in A.D. 64, this was attributed to the Christians. Some believed that Nero, the mad emperor sparked the devastating blaze. The historian Tacitus explained that his scapegoats were to be the Christians.

A development of far reaching consequences took place when the gospel of the early Palestinian Church was transplanted to the great cities of the Roman Empire. Before its ascendency, the soil was prepared, and the atmosphere conditioned for the rapid growth of the Church by the Greeks. The spread of the gospel was facilitated by the conquests of Alexander the Great which allowed many of the city states and small kingdoms of Europe and western Asia to increasingly come under the influence of the Greek culture. This dissemination of the Greek language and culture became historically known as the 'Hellenistic' culture. Thus "a common culture for all men was vigorously fostered in the numerous cities built by Alexander the Great and his successiors."[89] Hellenism began to spread in regions beyond Palestine and Western Asia by 200 B.C. The national cults, mysteries of Greece, the religious interpretation of life offered by the popular 'schools' of Greek philosophy, religions of Imperial Rome, the popular appeal of

---

89. James L. Price, Interpreting the New Testament., pg 108

oriental mystery religions, wide spread belief in astrology and magic, more speculative and mystical religions, all had their impact on the contemporary culture.

When the Greeks conquered the East, they practiced cults of their native city-states on foreign soil. With the establishment of the Hellenistic cities, efforts were made to worship Zeus, Hermes, Apollo, Artemis and other nationally known deities. However as the Greek city-states broke up, the honored gods vanished. The foreign gods were given the names of Roman deities, with the assumption that they were the same. Artemis worshipped at Ephesus, became the goddess of the mountain.

Early in the second century B.C. an attempt was made to revive the worship of the Homeric deities. Some festivals were added to the traditional calendar "but the pomp and circumstances of public worship failed to disguise the loss of a living faith."[90]

Following the death of Alexander, a sense of insecurity was felt everywhere. As Rome came into prominence the Emperor cult gave the Roman Army a feeling of pride in the military standards representing the soldierly virtues and so the veneration of the Emperor became an important aspect of the religion of cult and state. Anyone who refused to take part in simple ceremonies acknowledging the divine source of the benefits of Pax Romana (peace of Rome) was suspected of revolutionary activity.

As a result tensions developed between Christianity and Imperial Rome. As disciples spread the gospel throughout the Roman territories, it was inevitable that the Church became largely Gentile in membership and was recognized as a religious society distinct from Judaism. The Christian proclamation "Jesus Christ is Lord" easily became a treasonable statement. Roman Emperors, such as Caligula and Nero with the chief of them being Domitian, assumed the titles of Son of God, Savior, and Lord.

OTHER INFLUENCES ON GRECO-ROMAN CHRISTIAN CULTURE

The original *Sibylline Books* were introduced to Italy by Greek

---

90. Ibid., pg. 309.

colonizers. They were a collection of oracles from many 'Sibyls' or prophetesses. "In the fifth century B.C. a Sibylline oracle was observed and a temple was built in Rome to Demeter, Dionysius and Kore."[91] What survived after burnings, was often referenced by Christian fathers, and still is a repository of Gnostic, Judeo Christian beliefs and apocalyptic text.

Egyptian deities also influenced Greco-Roman ideas of deity. The God Osiris, Isis and their son Horus, were favored. Horus is associated with the sun and resurrection showing that the Egyptians worshipped a dying and rising god who offered men hope of a happy immortality. At Alexandria Greeks called their gods Sarapis or Osiris Hapi (Greek Osarapis), and gave him the attributes of Zeus, Hades and other Greek Deities. In-spite of repeated attempts to destroy Egyptian gods from 58-48 B.C., the cult was not denied.

In the pagan deity of the Greco-Roman world, Isis was probably the greatest. She was a friend of women, a wife, and a mother who understood suffering. Many features added to the popularity of Egyptian religion. Twice daily sacrifices, penitential practices, a continual round of duties performed by black-stoled priests in Isis' service, impressed observers of the reality of deities who were willing to enter into commerce with needy people. "Public ceremonies were regularly scheduled and at such times the image of Isis was displayed. The November festival was the passion and resurrection of Isis."[92a]

Worship of the god Mithras by Roman and Greek soldiers is often cited as inspiration for Jesus. People claim similarities in the birth, the twelve disciples or twelve zodiacs, and compare a banquet thrown by Mithras to the Last Supper. But Roman Mithraism post-dates Messianic prophesies by several centuries. It was carried to Britain, Germany and areas in the Roman Empire, and existed until A.D. 307, as evidenced by dedication of the Diocletian temple on the Danube River to Mithras.[92b]

---

91. Ibid., pg. 315.
92a.http://www.thedevineevidence.com/pagan_copycat_mithras.html
92b.http://www.mythencyclopedia.com/Mi-Ni/Mithras.html retrieved 12/23/13.

SPREAD OF CHRISTIANITY

The two outstanding leaders of the church, following the resurrection of Jesus were Peter and Paul.

PETER

Peter (from Greek, meaning "Rock") was the surname of that Simon, son of John and brother of Andrew, who originally was a fisherman near Capernaum. He became the first apostle of Jesus. His character vacillates between obstinate resolution and momentary cowardice as is shown in the story of the denial of his master. In Paul's story he appears as 'a pillar' of the primitive church and the apostle of the 'Circumcision'.

Peter is not mentioned in the Acts after the council at Jerusalem A.D. 50 but Galatians 2:11 refers to a subsequent visit by him to Antioch. His history after that incident has been overlaid with legends. He suffered martyrdom in Rome where he was crucified. Papal claims of primacy for Peter have appeared supported by Matthew 16:17-19.

PAUL

Saul of Tarsus was the son of Hebrew parents and belonged to the tribe of Benjamin. At the age of 13 he was most likely transferred to Jerusalem where his sister was, and there put under the charge of Gamaliel. Saul seems to have been led into deep antagonism to Christ and his cause and stood ready to undertake a crusade against the Christians. When Stephen earned the crown of martyrdom by being stoned to death, the young Saul did not hesitate to hold raiment of the witnesses who stoned him.

He obtained authority from the Chief priests to hunt down the Christians he persecuted and pursued his work of extermination. As he approached Damascus on his mission of persecution, he was overwhelmed by a dazzling splendor such as outshone the sun and heard a voice saying to him "Saul, Saul why persecutes thou me?" As a result he was struck with blindness. His sight was restored by Ananias and he was baptized and received the gift of the Holy Spirit.

He is then driven by the Holy Spirit into Arabia where he

spends a considerable time in meditation. The young Rabbi at Gamaliel's feet, becomes, at the feet of Christ the great teacher; translating Christianity into a universal religion.

Saul, who became Paul, went up to Antioch where he and Barnabas along with John Mark, were 'set apart' for missionary work. He made three missionary journeys through Asia Minor and Europe and the journey to Rome where he suffered martyrdom by beheading. There are thirteen epistles of St Paul in the New Testament which belong to the latter half of his ministry.

EXPANSION OF THE CHURCH

Constantine the Emperor of Rome became a convert of the Christian religion after previously worshipping the sun god. Before his military victories he saw a vision in the sun featuring the letters CH and R and the words "In hoc signo vinces" or 'in this sign shalt thou conquer'. He believed the message came from the Christian god, and with successes, he became the first Christian emperor. He turned the town of Byzantium into the great city of Constantinople and thus Christianity held an important stake in Eastern Europe and Asia. After Jerusalem and Rome, Constantinople became the third and most important city of Christendom.

The church was spreading throughout the world through the efforts of the Apostles. Christianity struggled to consolidate its power but before the religion, which now encompassed many races, nations and creeds could unify, it was split apart by bitter disputes. The topic that would rent the church in two was the confusing philosophical point about the relationship of Jesus to God. Was he divine or semi-divine? Has he always existed or was he created? If there was only one god what was the exact position of Jesus and the Holy Spirit in the celestial hierarchy?

The first general Council of the church met in A.D. 325 at the command of Constantine in an attempt to solve the row. The council had to deal with the heresy of Arianism. Arius questioned the divinity of Jesus, stating he was the highest being created but not divine. The result of this meeting was the Nicene Creed which sought to explain the role of Jesus the son, and was adopted as part of the Eucharist. An article known as the Filioque, dealt with the problem of the Holy Spirit by describing it as coming from the

"Father and the Son" rather than from the Father alone.

Constantinople was offended at the challenge to God's sole authority. In 457 A.D. the Council of Chalcedon was called. Five seats of authority were declared. They were at Constantinople, Rome, Jerusalem, Alexandria and Antioch. The Roman bishops saw themselves as descendants of St. Peter, and thus claimed moral ground. The bishop of Constantinople appointed himself the Title of Ecumenical Patriarch. The mutual distrust between the two centers continued to deepen however.

Another split came in the 6th century when the Monophysites found themselves isolated by their creed that there was "one nature" alone in Christ. They split to form the Syrian, Armenian and Coptic (Egyptian) churches. This led to further division within the Christian church.

ORTHODOX CHURCHES

In 1054 the patriarch of Constantinople was excommunicated. This came about because the Frankish king Charlemagne was crowned king by Pope Leo III in Rome and the influence of the Holy Roman Empire began to rise. Constantinople was eventually invaded by Muslims and Christianity was then reduced to a minor religion in that region. The Greek orthodox religion flourished and was exported with its immigrants. Consequently the eastern Orthodox Churches remained a separate federation with individual Patriarchs.

ROMAN CATHOLICISM

The fortunes of Rome ebbed and flowed in the first thousand years of Christendom. The glories of the Roman Empire, which began at the time of Jesus, ceded to invaders. Some like the Visigoths who struck in 410 were Christians by inclination, but most invaders who breached the borders of the empire were not.

Charlemagne, the Christian King of the Franks, did much to spread the word of Christianity. He offered the nationals of the countries he had invaded the opportunity to convert or die. Pope Leo was duly returned in glory to Rome and Charlemagne was crowned king of the Holy Roman Empire in A.D. 800.

When King John of England clashed with Pope Innocent III in 1205 over the posting of the Arch Bishop, England was placed under a six year edict which barred all church services. By the 13th century the clergy were straying from the teachings of Jesus, much as the Jews before them had lapsed from the laws of Moses. For centuries it was not unusual to find a Bishop with one or more mistresses, secreted away, and this was after they were supposed to have taken the vow of celibacy. Many lived in style, indulging in food and wines, showing barely a passing interest in society's outcasts who had so inspired Jesus.

There was also political division inside the church. The Roman Catholic Church had some 40 anti pope contenders to the title. With the ascendancy of France in the world's arena in the middle ages, French popes were elected. The Roman See (center) was based in France. From around 1309, the Catholic Church was focused there.

In 1378 Pope Urban VI left Avignon for the Vatican. The choice failed to unify the church and a body of Cardinals elected a second Pope- Clement VII to sit in France. Further confusion arose when a third pope declared himself in Prague. At the council of Constance in 1414 - 1418, the issue of pope of the Roman Catholic Church, along with many other issues, was resolved by choosing a compromise candidate Martin V who made Rome his seat.

THE ECUMENICAL CREEDS

The struggle between orthodoxy and heresy in the early church was not only the occasion for theological discussions of the fathers, but it also produced several creeds of ecumenical (universal) authority and significance. These documents grew out of deep conviction of faith and the instinct to utter publicly what was experienced personally. *A creed* (Latin Credo) 'I believe,' is a statement of confession of faith and belief.

"When Christ asked his disciples, "Who do you say that I am?" Peter replied, "You are the Christ, the Son of the Living God" as stated in Matthew 16:15-16. The creedal tradition was born. Subsequent affirmations and expansions of this Christo-centric Faith, on through the Trinitarian form, marks many creeds. The article on Jesus the Christ is not only central but normative. Creeds were used in many ways; as public statement on first becoming a Christian, on joining the church, as part of the liturgy of worship (to be recited or sung), as an ultimatum of the church against heresy, as a manifesto for unbelievers regarding what Christians believe."[93] There are four major creedal statements in the early church, one or more of which is still regarded as authoritative in both the Roman Catholic and Protestant Churches. These are:

1.   THE APOSTLES CREED

The Apostles creed which dates back to the earliest apostolic testimony about Jesus Christ and his relation to God the Father, the Holy Spirit, and the Church, is recited in Roman Catholic, Episcopalian and Protestant Churches. There was no single fixed form of the creed until late into the fifth century. Its brevity and conciseness contribute to its dominance among the western church (both Roman Catholic and Protestants). The Apostles Creed was frequently recited in Roman Catholic, Episcopalian and mainline Protestant churches as a part of their liturgy as follows:

"I believe in God, the Father Almighty,
maker of heaven and earth.
And in Jesus Christ his only son our Lord.
Who was conceived by the Holy Ghost,
Born of the Virgin Mary; suffered under Pontius Pilate,
was crucified, dead, and buried.
He descended into hell. The Third day he rose again from the dead.
He ascended into heaven,
And sits at the right hand of God the Father Almighty,
From thence he shall come to judge the quick and the dead.
I believe in the Holy Ghost (Spirit), the Holy Catholic Church,
the Communion of Saints, the forgiveness of sins.
The Resurrection of the body,
And the Life Everlasting. Amen." [94]

2.   THE NICENE CREED

In the east, the only authoritative creed was the statement

---

93. Hugh and Kerr, Writings in Christian thought. pg. 78.
94. Ibid., pg. 75.

prepared at the council of Nicea (A.D. 325) and revised at the council of Constantinople (A.D. 381), known simply as the Nicene Creed. "As a formally received document, it is thus older than the Apostles' Creed and has enjoyed more ecumenical acceptance that any other creed."[95] The occasion for the Nicene Creed was the unique dispute with the Arians over the definition of Christ's relation to God. The Arians in the interest of protecting the doctrine of Monotheism denied that Christ was the eternal son of God and asserted that he had been created and was not of the same substance or essence as the Father.

At the council of Constantinople some minor changes were made including an addition to the article on the Holy Ghost and the Arian anathema clause was omitted. This form of the Nicene Creed, sometimes called the Niceno-Constantinopolitan is the only one received by the Eastern orthodox churches. About the end of the sixth century, in the West, an addition was made in the statement about the Holy Ghost to indicate the "Double procession" of the Spirit from the Father and the Son (Filioque) and so it was thought the co-equality of the son with the Father could also be emphasized. This later version of the Nicene Creed is used in the West among Roman Catholic and Protestants.

3.   THE SYMBOL OF CHALCEDON

At the Council at Chalcedon in A.D. 451, assembled churchmen reaffirmed the existing Nicene Creed and added a more detailed analysis of the union and distinction of the human and divine natures of Jesus Christ. *__The Symbol of Chalcedon__*, as it is often called never had wide liturgical and catechetical use because of its complex language and intricate definition. But its importance, especially in the West was in the church's description of the limits of the orthodox doctrine of Christ's personhood. Four controversies provoked the Chalcedon Symbol (a) Arianism which denied the full deity of Church. (b) Apollinarianism which denied the full humanity of Christ. (c) Nestorianism which denied the union of the two natures.   (d) Eutychianism which denied the distinction of the two natures."[96]

---

95. Ibid., pg. 74.

4. THE ATHANASIAN CREED

The Athanasian Creed is important as an early statement on the subtleties of the doctrine of the Trinity and the relationship of the Father, Son, and Holy Spirit. The creed is attributed to the Athanasius, Bishop of Alexandria, the chief adversary against the Arians in the fourth century and so the "Father of Orthodoxy". The creed in its present form came much later, perhaps not earlier than the end of the eighth century. It echoes the Bishop of Hippo's Trinitarian position by stating both the co-equality of the three persons of the Trinity and at the same time their distinctions. This became a peculiar and much disputed feature of the Athanasian creed which restricted its use in the churches of the West especially in Protestantism.

THE REFORMATION

MARTIN LUTHER (1483 – 1546)

In 1517 Martin Luther produced his 95 Theses, which challenged the might of the Papacy, and nailed them to the door of the church at Wittenberg. Luther's aim was to stimulate internal reform in the church. There was an abuse of power by the Catholic Church. This was no dispute about heavenly matters or the nature of God and the Holy Spirit. The issues were earthbound and surrounded the manipulative interpretations of God's will by the Pope.

Martin Luther was a monk who found out that the sale of indulgences by the clergymen, in which sins were forgiven, was a bizarre distortion of Christian doctrine. He argued that man could reach heaven only through his personal faith. His message found a sympathetic hearing among lay people. In 1521 Luther was summoned to appear before the D.I.E.T. or assembly at Worms in southwest Germany. He was asked by the church authority to recant his Theses. He remarked – "Here I stand, I can do no less, God being by helper."

In 1534 Luther left the monastery at Wittenburg and a year later he married a former Cistercian Nun, Katherine Von Born.

---

96. Ibid., pg. 75.

They had six children. Not only did Luther stand up for his faith, but he became a rallying point for his people. Luther translated the Bible in German and was the author of some 42 hymns. The Lutheran denomination is a tribute to Luther. They became Luther's swan song. The main principles of the Reformation are:

- (a) The Scripture is the sole word of God and guide to faith
- (b) Justification is by faith alone.[97]
- (c) The Priesthood of all believers. (Every man is a

  priest to God)

ZURICH ZWINGLI (1484 – 1531)

Zwingli was a radical Swiss Church reformer who gave support to Luther. He argued whether Christ really was present in the bread broken at the Mass as Luther believed or whether the ritual of the Last Supper was purely symbolic.

JOHN CALVIN (1509 – 1564)

John Calvin was France's great reformer. He was a law and theology student who began campaigning for Protestantism in the 1530's. He tried to establish Protestantism in Geneva. In 1536 he was exiled from France. He saw Geneva as a Christian city formed to "Nourish and support the exterior service of God."

Calvin shared some of Luther's belief's. He believed in the authority of scripture and the importance of personal faith. His most famous works were the Institutes of the Christian Religion (1536) which lay down the rules for the Reformed Church and the Magnum Opus which was developed through a series of revisions until the final edition in 1559.

The Institutes were modeled on the sequence of the Apostle's Creed. However Calvin took liberties with the ancient formula of the creed and inserted long closely knit discussion on a variety of theological topics. He published commentaries on nearly every

---

97. Holy Bible, Romans 5:1.

book in the Bible, preaching constantly and carrying out a wide correspondence. Geneva was his main headquarters but for a time he also lived in Strasbourg which had become a shelter for French, German, English, and Scottish refugees.

Calvinism or the Reformed Faith moved from Switzerland into the Rhine Valley providing the theological impulse for the Huguenots in France, the Protestants in Holland, the Puritans of England and New England and the Presbyterians in Scotland and America. "The state churches of Holland and Scotland and some of the non-conformist churches in North America and Germany owe much to Calvinism."[98]

THE SOVERIGNTY OF GOD

Calvin was convinced from the scripture and his own experience that God is sovereign in the process of salvation- that it is God in Christ who takes the initiative in man's redemption, and that man has nothing whatever within him deserving of God's favor. "It was because he was so sure of the divine glory that he could speak of man's total depravity and predestination."[99]

The Bible is given by inspiration of God and is profitable for doctrine, for reproof, for correction, for instruction in righteousness, that the man of God may be perfect, thoroughly furnished with all good works (II Timothy 3: 16-17), became Calvin's thesis. He commends first, the authority of scripture, then the usefulness which proceeds from it. To Calvin our religion is different from all other in that the prophets have spoken, not of themselves, but as the instruments of the Holy Spirit.

The Reformation changed the thinking and beliefs of the people during the 16th century. Arising from the Reformation was the Evangelical revival in England and the Religious Awakening in the United States of America. Out of these came a desire to 1) restore primitive Christianity, and 2) to worship God on the dictates of conscience and freedom from oppression. The Religious Awakening was an invigorating, energizing influence on the

_____

98. Op. Cit., p. 161.
99. Hugh T. Kern, Readings in Christian Thought, pg 161.

church because it had become tied to forms and rituals, much to the neglect of the Holy Spirit.

JONATHAN EDWARDS (1703-1758)

Jonathan Edwards became the 'guiding light' of the Religious Awakening. The Presbyterian Church was sharply divided into Old lights and New lights. As a leader of the 'New lights' movement he spoke passionately. Many became evangelicals and took to the wild prairie with the good news of salvation. Soon, new churches and colleges were formed to instruct adherents. This led to the proliferation of universities and seminaries for the clergy, who would pastor new congregations.

Two ministers of the Presbyterian Church – Alexander Campbell and Barton Stone decided to establish a new denomination based on the restoration of primitive Christianity. They wanted to restore the church to its New Testament principles based on the sacrament of believer's baptism and the Lord's Supper-essentials of the Christian faith.

HENRY VIII (1491-1547) and THOMAS CROMWELL(1455-1540)

There was a different kind of reformation in England. Henry VIII (1491-1547) shaped the face of reformation in England. His chief advisor Thomas Cromwell (1455-1540) drew up a series of laws that made the monarch rather than the Pope the head of the church of England. When these laws did not work in Rome, Henry VIII all but abolished the influence of the Pope in England. In 1534 he passed the "*Act of Supremacy*" which enabled him to grant himself a divorce. The monasteries were dissolved, reducing many of England's finest buildings to rubble, and leaving destitute scores of poor people who had sought and found food and shelter from them.

Henry was married almost a quarter of a century to the widow of his elder brother Arthur. For years he had hoped for a son and heir but Catherine gave birth to only one child that lived, a girl called Mary. He applied to Rome for a divorce but was denied by the Pope. When an annulment wasn't granted the King defied the Pope and passed the act of Supremacy which enabled him to declare himself head of the protestant Church of England. Under

Elizabeth, his daughter with Anne Boleyn, the Protestant church developed. Colonization and the Act of Supremacy allowed the church to become a force to be reckoned with in England and throughout the British Empire.

The Reformation did not end divisions within the church. People of faith and reason began to question the practices of the church using reformation principles of scripture and the priesthood of all believers. They challenged the state church and denominations began to spring up. Some of these are: Methodists, Quakers, Congregationalists, Presbyterians, and Baptists. They accepted some of the practices of orthodoxy; for example, festivals or events like Advent, Christmas, Lent, Easter, Ascension Day, Pentecost on Whit Sunday, Trinity Sunday. The great emphasis was on the Eucharist (Lord's Supper/Holy Communion) and Baptism. Some free churches regard these two sacraments as ordinances.

FORMS OF WORSHIP IN VARIOUS FAITHS

Paul E. Johnson in Psychology of Religion presents a survey of worship in action that reveals the following forms in general use:

a) *The dance and procession* are seen as magnificent pageantry or ecstatic frenzy. Dances are employed by American Indians, people of African descent, whirling dervishes of the Semetic traditions, and Hindu worshippers of Siva and Rali. They dramatize tradition, prepare for expeditions, or induce excitement felt as divine possession. Processions are more evident in religious ceremonies. "A gold effigy of Osiris was daily presented to the setting sun, taken for a ceremonial voyage, or carried around the walls of Memphis, Egypt. In the New Year festival of Babylon, images of gods arrived from other temples like Anu from Erech and Enlil from Nippur. "To take the hands of the great Lord, Marduk."[100] Procession appeared in festivities of Greek mystery cults, Jewish pilgrimages to the temple and Moslem pilgrimage to the Mecca. In these and Christian church worship the procession signifies approaching the divine presence, progressing toward the

---

100. Paul E. Johnson, Psychology of Religion, pg 163

religious goal.

b) ***Invocation*** is the calling of a superior being to be present. It may be a vocal salutation, a request at the start of worship, or the invitation may be an artistic representation of the deity or seen in religious symbols. "Sketches and paintings of religious objects have been found discovered in Paleolithic caves of France, Spain, and Algeria. Sand paintings and Totem portrayal survive among America Indians. Models and carvings of images have wide religious use. Judaic, Muslim and sometimes Christian bodies have prohibited images, and turn to architecture rich in symbolism and eloquent in religious meaning. Altars, Pyramids, Obelisks, Minarets, and Mosques, Gothic arches and lofty Spires are invitations to meet God."[101]

c) ***Dramatic rituals*** seek to enact the events that are valued by the group. Myths and legends are dramatized to honor heroic exploits and ancestral spirits. "A ritual pattern in Egypt and Asia dramatized the death, resurrection, combat with enemies, sacred marriage and triumph of the god. Candles burning to signify the divine presence, incense to indicate the rising spirit of prayer, sacrifice and dedication are dramatic elements prevalent in many religions. The Roman Catholic Mass is a dramatic portrayal of the sacrificial work of Christ."[102]

Sacred music, vocal and instrumental, is widely used in worship. Rhythmic tom tom beats and vocal chants are used by Africans and American Indians. Wooden drums are used in Buddhist scriptural intonation and bells are common in China, India, Japan, European and American churches. All inspire worship and invite Deity to listen. The Hopi Indians conduct a nine day flute ceremony with prayers and offerings. Psalms and laments have been sung in Hebrew worship from the Exodus till now. The chorus was prominent in Greek tragedies - celebrating religious mythology. "Christian choral music has developed stirring harmonies that with congregational singing express the emotions of profound worship."[103]

---

101. Ibid. pg. 164.
102. and 103. Ibid., pg. 164.

d) **Prayer** is an act of worship that takes many forms. Mechanical devices such as prayer wheels, placing prayers in wells, waves, fires are used but these are little more than incantations. Prayers are marked by fixation of attention by posture, closed eyes, controlled gaze, or rosary to avoid distraction, and concentrating wholly on the Divine being. Prayers may be called out in a loud voice to attract the deity or a vigil of silence to create intimate communion. "Prayer is the heart of worship. Without divine visitation and communion worship is not complete."[104]

e) **Sacrifice** has been practiced in worship of most religions. The Hebrews offered the first fruits of the harvest and the flock in gratitude for divine blessings. The Vedic Aryans poured melted butter on the fire. Romans made a libation of wine. Brahmins offered horse sacrifices. Followers of Mithra sacrificed a bull. Human sacrifices were offered by the Aztecs and Maoris. Offerings express gratitude or petition, expiate sin, dedicate for sacramental use, seal vows and covenants. "To Christians the crucifixion of Jesus is a vicarious sacrifice for the sins of the world, reconciling God and man. The Jewish Passover and the Christian sacrament of Holy communion (Eucharist) are feasts to recreate spiritual life."[105]

f) **Confession and purification** recognize the evils of life and seek to dispose of them. Various cultures have their own acts of confession. Japanese, Egyptian, Greeks, Hindus resort to Lustrations. The Celts, Romans and Persians use fire as a purifying energy. "The Hebrews heap the sins of the people upon a scapegoat driven into the wilderness. Navajo chant for the removing of evil or illness, requiring an elaborate use of prayer sticks, plumed wands, paddles, snake sticks, ashes, powder, feather, jewels, reeds, rush offerings, arrows, whistles, bullroarers, flints, clubs, tokens, rattles and medicines. Confession of sins brings the purification to a higher level of repentance, forgiveness and renewal."[106]

---

104. Ibid. pg. 164.
105. Ibid., pg. 165.
106. Ibid. pg. 161.

g) *Recitation* forms a natural part of worship. No people are without cherished traditions unique to their heritage. The reciting of these traditions is significant for the instruction of the young and for the interpretation of customs and events. "Mythology is the philosophy of primitive man attempting to answer the mysterious questions of creation, nature, life, and destiny."[107]Every mature society has its bible to preserve the words of life, the true teachings and history of the faith. Sacred scriptures are accepted as divine revelation to be heeded and followed by all who profess the Faith. Professing the faith brings the creed to a lofty place in worship as the affirmation and avowal of the faithful. For example – the Synagogue service of the Jews opens with the Shema and calls upon laymen to come forward and read from the Torah. Moslems listen with rapt attention to the reciting of the Koran.

Christian worship gives a large place to reading and preaching from the Bible. "By meditating upon the inspired word, sacred traditions are enshrined in living personalities and come to new birth through the labors of many minds."[108] Divergent as these forms of worship appear, they converge into a clear pattern of unity. Coming from every time and place of human habitation, these varieties of aspirations have a common center. They all point to God, who cares and responds to the needs of persons.

Worship is a reverent outreach of the human spirit toward THOU with ultimate concern. To the Christian that THOU is God the Father Almighty seen through Jesus Christ the only begotten son and the Holy Spirit that proceeds from the Father. We now speak of the Triune God or the Holy Trinity.

---

107. Ibid., pg. 165.
108. Ibid., pg. 163.

Chapter 9

THE DEVELOPMENT OF FAITH THROUGH RELIGIOUS SYMBOLS, DEVOTION, AND DOCTRINE

In the middle ages, Christianity was visual. Architecture, windows, ornaments, tapestries, paintings, tombs all represented Faith. All of these carried stories. This is not so with mid-western Protestantism. Patricia S. Klein in Worship without Words describes her awe at this difference like this; "For the first time in my life I encountered the reliquary and the triptych (not to be confused with the AAAS Trip-tick), I could touch and see the symbols of faith in stone and fabric and metal."[109]

She describes her visit to the Cloister in New York City where she found herself immersed in what seemed to be an entire language. She also discovered the tapestry of the Apostle's Creed. "On the wall of one of the corridors, hung a beautiful tapestry in which the entire creed was woven in symbols."She described how she studied the words of the creed, imprinting on her soul a visual memory of the ancient words that she had only recently began to include in her weekly worship. "I began a new journey into a worship experience that was not dependent upon words. My faith from childhood had been always rooted in words, specifically the word of God or the Bible."[110]

The history of Christian worship is bathed in symbolism, beginning with symbols from Jewish scriptures. These are: The rainbow God gave Noah, the bronze serpent that Moses raised to bring healing, and the Passover meal which established a memorial to God's rescue of the Israelites from Egypt. Jesus himself understood the importance of symbols in his own worship and in his teachings; "Just as Moses lifted up the serpent in the wilderness, I am the bread of life, I am the light of the world, I am the good shepherd, I am the vine" (John 8, 9, and 10). In His final meal with his disciples he established a memorial for those who

---

109. Patricia S. Klein., Worship Without Words, The sign and Symbols of our Faith, pg. 1X.
110. Ibid. pg. 1X-X.

love him in the institution of the Lord's Supper

God uses physical things to communicate the transcendent and knowable things, to communicate the unknowable. God's gifts us with the world and our physical nature. Because we are physical creatures our worship is filled with signs and symbols. The symbols of Faith and worship remind, they teach, they translate God into our everyday experience. "Indeed these are sacraments which according to the Book of Common Prayer are outward and visible signs of inward and spiritual grace."[111]

Christianity spread from Rome throughout Europe, converting people of many languages and cultures. However, literacy was limited in the Middle Ages and the Reformation. Worship was done in Latin. Worship literacy was therefore limited to those who could understand Latin. It was in this environment that colors, gestures, and symbols, became the language of worship. One did not need to read in order to understand what was happening in the Mass. It became possible to worship without words.

Most liturgical traditions (language, gestures, symbols, prayers, responses of priest and people) of the western church are anchored in the church of Ancient Rome. In the middle ages *Monasticism* (setting oneself apart from the world as in a Monastery), became an integral part of the church. Priests and Monks led worship, transcribed scripture and participated in liturgy. Patricia Klein states "The model of liturgical churches is not democracy but monarchy. To modern minds this is an unsavory concept. If monarchy defined the appearance of the church, Monasticism defined the substance of worship, setting forth the disciplines, the values and practices, of daily worship and life in Christ. Monarchy and Monasticism together characterize most aspects of liturgical life today. For Protestants who moved away from liturgical worship with the advent of the Reformation, worship practices have become more of the peoples own making or choice."

THE SYMBOLS AND WHAT THEY CONVEY IN WORSHIP

1. God is present at the altar in all of His Holiness and

---

111. Ibid. pg. X.

'otherness', in the elements of the Eucharist. ***The Altar*** is the center of the liturgical worship and is a sign of the presence of God in the Holy Eucharist. The Roman Catholic churches differ theologically regarding the substance of the bread and wine. All acknowledge the Eucharist as the central memorial of Christ's sacrifice for us, and the altar as the table on which this memorial is celebrated.

"The Altar is not simple furniture; the sanctuary is not merely space. God is present at the Altar and His presence fills the sanctuary, just as He was present in the Holy of Holies. The presence of God in the Eucharist and at the Altar is the key to understanding many other aspects of liturgical worship and practice."[112]

2. ***Baptism***.-(from Greek- to dip, to immerse). This is the second liturgical symbol of faith. Baptism is a defining moment of Faith in ones religious experience. It is the beginning of one's membership in the body of Christ. In many non liturgical churches more emphasis is placed on the profession of faith- accepting Christ as personal savior. Baptism is the public act subsequent to that profession. Baptism is celebrated in the name of the Father, and of the Son, and of the Holy Spirit (Matthew 28:19) thus admitting the baptized one into the body of Christ – the Church.

Believer's Baptism- The sacrament is offered by those churches who affirm that baptism is available only for those who have made profession of faith in Jesus Christ. In these churches it is the profession that admits a believer into the church, and baptism is the subsequent public seal of that baptism.

Christening – is another term for baptism particularly of infants and children, "that emphasizes becoming a member of God's family and being given a name that is proclaimed to the entire community. Churches that do not practice infant baptism often have similar services for infants which they call dedication."[113] This is the commitment of child to God by the parents, who promise to bring up the child in the faith and offer the child to the

---

112. Ibid. pg. X11.
113. Ibid. pg. 112.

service of God. (Samuel 1:27-28).

FORMS OF BAPTISM

Affusion- Water is poured or sprinkled on the head of the person being baptized as the blessing is pronounced. A Font is used for this form of Baptism. Another form of affusion is known

as Immersion. In this process, the one being baptized stands in the water with part of the body being submerged (usually to the waist). Water is then poured over the rest of the body as the blessing is pronounced.

Submersion- The candidate is totally covered by the water of baptism, laid backwards into the water while being supported by the Officiate. Some traditions call for a single submersion, some for three. Submersion is reminiscent of death to old life and resurrection into new life in Christ (Romans 6:4, Colossians 2:12).[114]

In Protestant denominations this form of baptism is referred to as immersion. A tank or pool is sometimes provided in the church for this purpose (Baptistery). Some churches prefer to use a natural body of water i.e. a River or the Sea.

3. *The Sacraments.*-(Sacramentum in Latin) A Sacrament was an oath of allegiance of the Emperor, evidenced by the branding on the soldiers' arm or forehead in ancient times. The word Sacramentum was first introduced into Christian vocabulary by Tertullian (third century) who spoke of Baptism as a consecration through oath and visible sign (brand) made possible through the Paschal mystery of Christ or his incarnation, death, and resurrection.[115] The Latin Vulgate later translated the Greek word "mystery" using the word Sacramentum. Mystery is used in the New Testament to describe God's hidden plan manifested throughout human history now made accessible through the Holy Spirit to those who have faith. (Matthew 13:11, Romans 16:25-26 Ephesians 3:4-5).

---

114. Ibid. pg. 112.
115. Ibid. pg 110.

Early Christians regarded Baptism and the Lord's Supper as the rites that expressed both faith and obedience toward God. They are visible representations of redemption. Augustine described a sacrament as a sacred sign or "visible word" comprised both of word and physical elements. Sacrament is later described in the Book of Common Prayer as "an outward and visible sign of an inward and spiritual grace."

In the twelfth century the sacraments expanded from Baptism and Lord's Supper to include as many as thirty. By the time of Thomas Aquinas and the Council of Trent, only seven sacraments were affirmed by the Church. The Reformation further defined and distilled the meaning of sacraments for Protestants. Virtually all Christians recognize Baptism and the Eucharist (Lord's Supper) as Sacraments instituted by Christ.

SACRED PLACES, SACRED SPACES

Patricia Klein divides Ecclesiastical buildings into two classes – (a) Churches and (b) Oratories.

a) *Church* – a house of God, dedicated exclusively for public worship. A sacred building dedicated to divine worship for the use of all the faithful and the public exercise of religion. There are five kinds of churches.

1) *Cathedral* – The chief church of a diocese where the bishop's throne (or Cathedral which is the Latin word for "sent") is situated.

2) *Collegiate* – or Conventual – a public place of worship served by a community of regular clergy, (Canons, regular Monks or Friars).

3) *Metropolitan* – A Church presided over by an Archbishop.

4) *Parochial* – A Parish Church with a Baptismal font, a confessional, and a Cemetery, and the liturgical equipment necessary for baptisms, marriages and funerals.

(b) *Oratory* – is a place of worship not intended for the use of the faithful indiscriminately. These can be a public oratory which is used by a religious community primarily with limited access by the public, a semi – public oratory which is intended for use by a special community and is not open to the public, and a private oratory which is a small chapel or room set apart for worship in a private house for the use of the family or an individual. There are other ecclesiastical structures (oratories-sacred spaces) such as:

1) *Catacomb* – an underground cave or tunnel the early Christians used for burial and as a meeting place during the time of Roman persecutions.

2) *Manse* – The residence of the clergy, particularly in the Presbyterian (Reformed Church). It may also be called Parsonages, Rectory, Vicarage or Presbytery.

3) *Mission* – An establishment of missionaries which may include a church, a school, a hospital and other facilities from which the missionaries do outreach work. It may also refer to a local parish.

4) *Shrine* – A building or other shelter that encloses the remains or relics or a saint or other holy person, becoming the site of religious veneration and pilgrimage.

SACRED ARCHITECTURE

a) *Cruciform* – Cross shaped Churches which have a Nave, Transept, and Chancel. The formation from above takes the shape of a Latin Cross.

b) *Gothic* – An ornate style of architecture of Europe in the middle ages (12th century). Distinguishing features are pointed arches, ribbed vaulting and slender spires. Examples – The Rheims and Notre Dame Cathedrals.

c) *Romanesque* – A style of architecture based on Roman building techniques, prevalent in Europe from the fifth century to the 12th. The distinctive features are the round arch and the barrel (or tunnel vault). It is unadorned and massive.

d) *The Cross* – The Cross is the central furnishing of an Altar, symbolizing atonement and humankind's redemption. Above all, the Cross is the central symbol of the Christian Faith. Patricia Klein remarked that it is hard to imagine a hangman's noose or an electric chair as an object of worship and veneration. Quoting Dorothy L. Sayers, she observed "it is curious that people who are filled with horrified indignation whenever a cat kills a sparrow, can hear the story of the killing of God told Sunday after Sunday and not experience any shock at all."[116]

Looking beyond his death, Jesus once told a crowd of Jews and visiting Greeks, "I, when I am lifted up from the earth, will draw all people to myself" (John 12:32). He understood that it was through the Cross that God would be glorified and that all people would be reconciled to his holiness. Early Christians realized that following Jesus Christ meant embracing the Cross. Paul wrote to the Galatian Christians I have been crucified with Christ and I no longer live, but Christ lives in me (Galatians 2:20). May I never boast except in the Cross of our Lord Jesus Christ, through which the world has been crucified to me and I to the world (Galatians 6:14). Through this instrument of death has come life. Life as it can flow only from God, fresh vibrant and unending.

This hymn from the liturgy of St. James acknowledges the profound dichotomy from the Cross of Jesus Christ.

"Let all mortal flesh keep silence
and stand with fear and trembling
pondering nothing earthly minded
by many-eyed Cherubim
and six winged Seraphim
who cover their faces chanting
Allelula, Allelula, Allelula."[117]

e) *The Pulpit*

The Pulpit or from the Latin, 'raised platform' is the place from which the sermon is delivered. It is located at the front of the Church. It is raised so that the persons speaking may be easily seen by the congregation. It may be octagonally shaped, symbolic of the regeneration of the spirit by the word of God. After the

---

116. Ibid. pg. 28.
117. Ibid. pg. 29

Reformation, the pulpit became centered in the Sanctuary. It is symbolic of the word of God as the scripture became the central focus of free worship in the church. Preaching became central in Evangelical worship.

f) *The Lectern*

The word in Latin means 'to read'. The Lectern is a wooden or metal desk from which the Bible lessons are read. The Lectern may be used instead of the pulpit for preaching in lesser services. The Lectern is not prominent in the evangelical sanctuary. In some of them, it is not found. Both pulpit and lectern create a divided Chancel in the Roman Catholic and Anglican or Episcopalian Churches. This is sometimes found in churches in other denominations.

THE LITURGICAL YEAR

Time is to be sanctified like everything else by the presence and action of Christ. Consequently, the Church has devised the Liturgical year with special days, seasons and colors to be used in worship. Major events of the birth and development of Christianity are marked by the two advents of Christ; his first coming in humility and obscurity, the second coming in majesty and power. These have been claimed by God for his own people.

The Church year is arranged in two large divisions; - first the festival portion commemorating the life and work of Jesus Christ and the second is the non-festival portion which sets forth the standards of the Christian life.

SEASONS OF THE CHURCH YEAR

The five seasons of the Church year are: Advent, Christmas, Lent, Paschal Triduum (A three day season that begins at sundown on Holy Thursday and may end either at Easter Vigil or at sundown Easter Sunday), and Easter (Easter runs through Pentecost Sunday). The time of the year that is not associated with the five seasons of the church year is known as Ordinary time.

Ordinary time is divided into two groups: Ordinary Time 1 and Ordinary Time 2 . The first group (Ordinary Time 1) falls between the seasons of Christmas and Lent. "In the Anglican and Protestant traditions this season is known as the season of Epiphany."[118]

The second group (Ordinary time 2) begins with Trinity Sunday (the Sunday after Pentecost Sunday) and runs through the feast of Christ the King (the last Sunday of the Church year). This season is sometimes known as the Trinity season and in the Anglican and Protestant traditions may be known as the season of Pentecost.

COLORS OF THE CHURCH YEAR

Liturgical colors change with the seasons of the Ecclesiastical year and serve as visual reminders of the nature of the season being celebrated. The colors appropriate to the season appear in the Paramounts (Paraments) of the Altar, Pulpit, and Lectern and in the celebrants stole Maniple and Chasuble. The colors are:

BLACK

Black: signifying mourning and death. Black is used on Good Friday and also may be used on Ash Wednesday and also in Masses and offices of the dead.

BLUE

The color of hope; Blue has recently been recognized as an alternate to the liturgical purple.

GOLD

Gold may be used as the liturgical color on Easter (instead of White) to give emphasis to the most holy day of the church year. It is also appropriate for the Last Sunday after Pentecost – the feast of Christ the King.

GREEN

The liturgical color symbolizing penitence and mourning; used during the two penitential seasons of Advent and Lent.

---

118. Ibid. pg. 37.

RED

The liturgical color symbolizing love and zeal bringing to mind fire and blood is used on Palm Sunday, Good Friday, and for celebrations of the Passion. It is also used on Pentecost, the day on which the Holy Spirit descended, appearing in tongues of fire, and since this day is recognized as the birthday of the Christian Church.

WHITE

The liturgical color symbolizing purity and joy is used at Christmas and Easter and the non passion Feast of the Lord – The presentation and the Annunciation – (the Visitation).

THE STAINED (COLORED) GLASS WINDOW

This is a medieval product that adorned the Church in order to convey to the worshipers through art the Faith principle. Some of these are paintings of: Jesus praying in the Garden of Gethsemane, Lamb of God, The Madonna, and Jesus as the Shepherd. I recall that the church in which I grew up had a colored glass window at the back of the Chancel and Choir stall. In it was inscribed the painting of Jesus as the Good Shepherd with the shepherd's crook in His hand. It indicates He is seeking out and protecting the sheep. The message conveyed to me reinforced the story of the Good Shepherd in Psalm 23, and the story that Jesus told of himself being the Good Shepherd that lays down his life for the sheep. I was that sheep for whom he died.

SIGNIFICANCE OF RELIGIOUS PAINTINGS

Many paintings exist which show biblical scenes or interpretations of scenes from the Bible while others highlight scriptures. They are used to tell a story pictorially or to give an artist's interpretation of a scripture or to Inspire. There are many famous religious painting in Churches and sold separately to hang in one's home. One such painting hangs over my bed in my bedroom. There is therapeutic value derived from the message in the painting. The history of this painting dates back to 1963, the year of our marriage.

Shortly after our marriage, the secretary of the church, which I pastured in Kingston Jamaica, presented us with this painting which she had done. It is a beautiful depiction of a vase filled with a stunning arrangement of flowers. She was an Art and Craft teacher at the Greenwich All Age School where I also was manager. The Calligraphy at the base of the painting illustrated that the artwork was inspired by Isaiah 40:31. "They that wait upon the Lord shall renew their strength; they shall mount up with wings as eagles. They shall run, and not be weary, and they shall walk and not faint."

My wife tells the story that during her recent bout of cancer, this painting came alive to her in her meditations on its message. She drew strength from the beauty of the painting, its execution, the beauty of the calligraphy and the poetry of the words and their meaning. She attributed much of her healing to the inspiration she drew from the words. Indeed, her faith became emboldened and to a great extent the words of scripture helped the healing process. Today she is cancer free. She waited on God and He healed her physically and spiritually. It is remarkable how faith can be strengthened by symbols.

DEVOTION - PRAYERS OF THE PEOPLE

THE GENERAL INTERCESSIONS

Intercession is to pray on behalf of others. The general intercessions are otherwise called Prayers of the faithful or Prayers of the People. There is a time of prayer or intercession in the liturgy in which the needs of the congregation, the church, and the world are brought before God, (1Timothy 2:1-2). These usually take the form of a litany in which the Officiants offer a specific request and following a time of silence for individual prayer, the people respond in accordance with the form used.[119] These prayers may also be called Bidding Prayers in the Anglican tradition.

INVOCATION (Latin root 'vocare'- to call upon)

The announcement at the beginning of the service invoking God's presence is known as the Invocation. For example; a call

---

119. Ibid. pg. 83.

such as: 'In the name of the Father and the Son, and the Holy Ghost (Spirit)' is really a prayer invoking the blessing of God.

LITANY

A Litany is an intercessory prayer. It is a form of prayer however, in which the petitions are uttered by the Pastor. The Congregation responds with a refrain after each statement, such as 'hear us O Lord'. The oldest form of litany is the Kyrie Eleison (Lord have mercy upon us).

THE LORD'S PRAYER

The prayer of Christ taught disciples as the model prayer. Matthew 6: 9-13, Luke 11: 2-4. It is used at almost every service in traditional churches. It has become the best known and most beloved Christian prayer in the world. It contains the new formulation doxology (used by the free church).

SILENT PRAYERS

These are the worshipper's private devotions before and after service.

THANKS GIVING

These involve the offering of praise to God for his goodness and mercy. Patricia Klein in 'Worship without Words,' quotes Romano Guardini on prayer in the following: "Prayer is a profound act of worship that asks neither why nor wherefore. It rises like beauty, like sweetness, like love. The more there is in it of love the more sacrifice. And when the fire has wholly consumed the sacrifice, a sweet savor ascends"[120]

INDIVIDUAL PRAYER

One does not need to be totally dependent on the worship of the church to develop one's faith. In prayer one communicates with God and His son Jesus Christ our Savior. It is hoped that as one matures in the faith even so will one's prayer life develop.

---

120. Ibid. pg. 84.

Individual prayers may be centered on one's situation. "Prayer is to entreat or petition. It is a supplication solemnly addressed to God. It is offered in the spirit of humility and is accompanied usually by adoration and confession, thanksgiving and supplication."[121] The living religions of the world place great emphasis on the spirituality of their adherents. An important aspect of this is prayer, meditation and fasting.

Those of us who are Christians have grown to appreciate prayer and its impact on our lives. Our Priest/Pastor, Elder, parents and other individuals have prayed for us. Many of us have been nurtured through the prayer meetings of our Church, and consequently have placed a high premium on prayer. We pray daily and can testify to the blessings we derive from praying to God our Father.

In praying we talk with God. We must know who He is and have faith in Him before we can talk or communicate with Him. We know God through His revelation in Jesus Christ and the created order. To have faith in God is to have faith in Jesus Christ but faith is not a magic word. Faith is belief in God, His son Jesus Christ and the teaching and doctrines of the church. In exercising our faith in God through prayer, we receive healing and are restored to health. We are reconciled to God and our neighbors, and find peace with God. It is this peace with God that results from communicating with Him through prayer and meditation. "Prayer is a heart to heart talk between yourself and God, and needs no brilliant ideas, no flood of words"[122] – as stated in The Jerusalem Community Rule of Life.

Debra K. Farrington refers to three aspects of prayer, relating to God, hearing from God, telling God our deepest desires. Finally she mentions this should be done without ceasing. The time we spend in prayer deepens our relationship with God. Prayer is also a time for hearing the Truth. Prayer times are opportunities to tell God what is on our minds and hearts. There are as many ways,

---

121. Rev. Dr. Leslie Seaton, Lord Teach Us To Pray. Pg. 8.
122. Debra K. Farrington. Living Faith Day by Day, pg. 56.

places, and times to pray as there are individuals in this world. Debra K. Farrington cites the following guidelines for individual prayer:

1) Set aside a place for prayer. One does not need to go to a church in order to have that experience. Just as Monks and Nuns have a chapel located within the monastery in which they live, we too can create a prayer corner or altar in our home that becomes a sacred, prayer space for us. A prayer corner in a room set aside for prayer can be as simple or as elaborate as you choose. Try following these simple steps to enhance your prayer time.

2) Make the space a private one if you are able- a place where you can close yourself off from family members, roommates or other people.

3) Provided it is possible, dedicate this space to prayer.

4) Clear the space of distractions if you can. Remove telephones, fax machines, pagers, loud clocks, or anything else that would disturb your prayers.

5) Have something comfortable on which to sit - a chair, couch, mat, pillow, that supports your body and does not cut off circulation, (i.e. A prayer stool or kneeler), candles, devotional or prayer book, the Bible, religious work of art, flowers, any object that helps you pray.

6) Pray regularly in this space- making it your holy ground.

7) "The first time you pray in your new prayer corner take a few moments to invite God into this space most particularly. Just as you might spend time with a good friend in a favorite coffee shop, restaurant or on a park bench, this space is one in which you will spend time with God."[123]

SILENCE IN PRAYER

Another aspect of Faith and Prayer is to practice silence. One of the most important and often the most difficult parts of prayer is

---

123. Ibid. pg. 57.

learning to be silent and listen to God. Silence is harder to maintain than a balanced conversation. Close your eyes and try to be perfectly still for even thirty seconds without your attention drifting off. Unless you have had some training in this area, chances are you noticed several thoughts crossing your mind in those thirty seconds. The world in which we live does not encourage or reward silence. It is very hard to hear God guiding us when we are afraid of silence. Learning to be silent is no different from developing strong muscles. It takes practice.

Farrington suggest different methods that can be employed to help quiet the chatter in your mind:

a. Sit in a comfortable position, close your eyes and focus on your breathing. Imagine that you are breathing in the grace and love of God and breathing out all of your concerns, frustrations and worries.

b. Sit in a comfortable position with your eyes open. Focus your attention on a devotional object of your choice – a candle, something in nature, or whatever reminds you of God's presence. Use the object as a focus, clearing your mind of other thought. Let the object speak to you of God."[124]

PRAY WITHOUT CEASING

This may be a good suggestion for a hermit who has nothing else to do in this world. It may sound impossible for busy people. Praying without ceasing does not mean that we sit cross-legged praying a mantra twenty four hours a day, seven days a week. We pray without ceasing when we try to remain conscious of God's presence throughout the day by constantly returning our focus to God. In Monasteries and Convents, this is done in part, by observing regularly scheduled periods of prayer all through the day and even well into the night in some places. Monks or Nuns gather to pray at Services established for that particular time of the day or evening. The practice allows the participants focus to return regularly to God.

To learn to pray without ceasing use your daily activities as a

---

124. Ibid. p. 62-65.

springboard for prayer, begin by making a list of things to do in a given day. Learning to become aware of God's presence continually, like any other discipline, requires some practice. Try to avoid criticizing yourself for not being able to master praying without ceasing instantly. Give yourself time to develop the practice. Try to see God in everything and everyone. Form a habit of continually talking with God and refer all you do to Him. "After a little care His love brings us to it without any difficulty."[125]

THE MUSIC OF WORSHIP

The music of Christian worship grew out of the music of Jewish worship, resplendent with Psalms and Hymns from the scriptures. Paul encouraged the Ephesians to be filled with the Spirit, speak to one another with psalms, hymns and spiritual songs, "sing and make music in your heart to the Lord, always giving thanks to God the Father, for everything, in the name of the Lord Jesus Christ."[126] Among the oldest sacred songs still used in the church today are Psalms and Canticles- the music from the scriptures.

CANTICLES (Latin word 'canticulum/ cantus' - little Song)

A Canticle is a sacred song or prayer, usually from biblical text, other than one of the psalms from the Bible is often used in liturgical worship. Old testament canticles include the two canticles of Moses; Exodus 15: 1-18, Deuteronomy 32: 1-43, the Canticle of Habakkuk; Hab. 3: 2-19, the Canticle of Isaiah; Isaiah 12: 2-6, the Canticle of Hezekiah: Isaiah 38:10-20, the Canticle of Hannah: 1Samuel 2:1-10. The three New Testament Canticles are: the Benedictus, Nunc Dimittis, and the Magnificat, and are all taken from the gospel of Luke.

BENEDICTUS (Latin meaning -"Blessed").

This is sometimes called the song (or canticle) of Zechariah for these are the words of Zechariah, the father of John the Baptist, found in Luke 1: 68-79.

---

125. Ibid. p. 71.
126. The Holy Bible, Revised Standard Version Ephesians 5: 18-20.

MAGNIFICAT (Latin meaning- "Magnify")

The words are those of the Virgin Mary to Elizabeth, found in Luke 1: 46-55. This Canticle sometimes is called the song (or canticle) of Mary and is sung in Vespers in orthodox Catholic churches.

NUNC DIMITTIS (Latin-meaning 'Now you are dismissing your servant')

The words are those of Simeon at the presentation of the infant Jesus at the Temple, found in Luke 2: 29-32. The Canticle is sung daily in Vespers or during evening prayer in the Anglican Church/Episcopalian Church.

THE GREGORIAN CHANT

This is chanted on eight tones with dignity and in unison with the text, determining the rhythm. It is named after Gregory the Great (Seventh Century) who wrote a collection of chants called "Antiphonar" and lent his name to the Latin rite that would later become the rite celebrated in most Western Europe.

MUSIC OF THE REFORMATION

A significant feature of the Reformation was the increase in the availability of scripture and scriptural knowledge among the laity. What was once the province of Clergy, now is available to the congregation. This was no less true in the realm of Church music. Martin Luther who was instrumental in restoring hymn singing to the congregation affirmed, "I place music next to theology and give it the highest praise."[127]

The years following the Reformation were rich in the creation of Christian music by composers such as Georg Frederick Handel, Sebastian Bach, and Felix Mendelssohn and hymn writers such as Charles Wesley, John Newton, and Isaac Watts. Anthems, Carols, Chorale, Chorus and Gospel Music, also played an important part in the worship of the Church and the strengthening of the Faith.

---

127. Patricia S. Klein pg. 108.

Patricia Klein in making reference to John Calvin writes, "In truth we know by experience that song has great force and vigor to move and inflame the hearts of men to invoke and praise God with a more vehement and ardent zeal." She further states that Martin Luther wrote "I am not satisfied with those who despise music, gift of God, no gift of other persons. It also drives away the devil and makes people cheerful. One forgets all anger, un-chasteness, pride, and other vices."[128]

Gospel music has emerged recently especially among African American Churches and white rural churches in America's South. This is uniquely American Christian music with roots in the rural south. It consists of a blend of intricate harmonies, energizing rhythms and blues sound. This kind of music is commonly associated with the Negro Spirituals. Listed here are some of the great hymns of faith. The reader can find them in many hymnals and African American hymn books. To read the entire hymn will reveal its theology and message and the period in which it was written.

1) *Hymns*:

Abide with me, fast falls the eventide.
Amazing Grace, how sweet the sound.
And can it be, that I should gain.
Beneath the Cross of Jesus.
Faith of our Fathers.
He leadeth me, O blessed thought.
Immortal Invisible, God only wise.
Lead us heavenly Father, lead us.
Love divine, all love's excelling.
My Faith looks up to Thee
O for a thousand tongues to sing my great Redeemer's praise.
Praise my Soul, the King of Heaven.
Praise to the Lord, the Almighty the King of Creation.
What a friend we have in Jesus.
When I survey the Wondrous Cross.

---

128. Ibid., pg. 140.

2) *Oratorios*:

Handel's Messiah
Verdi's Requim

3) *Classical Solos*:

Agnes Dei – (Lamb of God)
Ave Maria
Ave Verum
How lovely are Thy dwellings O Lord
Know Ye the Lord of Hosts
Open the gates of the Temple
Panis Angelicus
The Lord is my Light and Salvation
The Prayer of St. Fancis (Make me an instrument of your Peace)

4) *Chants*:

Te Deum Laudamus
The Gregorian Chant

INSTRUCTIONS OF THE FAITH

THE CATECHISM

This is a book of instruction explaining the Ten Command-ments, the Creeds, the Sacraments and the Lord's Prayer. It is used in teaching Christian doctrine, especially to those preparing to become members of the church.

The Heidelberg and Geneva Catechism of the Reformed Church are among the more familiar Catechism. Luther's larger and smaller Catechisms (Lutheran Church) and the Anglican Catechism called "an outline of the Christian Faith," are found in the in the Book of Common Prayer. The Roman Catholic Catechisms have revised and updated several times, ranging from the Baltimore Catechism (1885), the Catechism of the Catholic Church (1992) to The Compendium of the Catechism (2005) and YouCat, a catechism for youth in 2011.

DOCTRINE

The Apostles Creed is a statement of faith summarizing the doctrines taught by the Apostles dating back to about A.D. 500. It is the shortest and best known Creed. The Creed is rooted in the Old Roman Creed, with early evidence of it being used in baptismal rites as an interrogatory Creed. The Creed was broken into three sections. God, Jesus Christ, one Holy Spirit, then presented to the initiate as a question that began with "Do you believe, to which the response is "I do" or "I believe".

PROLIFERATION OF THE CHURCH AND OTHER CREEDS

There are other Creeds that are used sometimes in the Roman Catholic and Episcopalian Churches. They are (a) *The Nicene Creed* which is the confession of Faith drawn up by the council of Nicaea in 325 A.D. and commonly used in the Communion Service and on feast days. (b) *The Creed of Saint Athanasius*. This is the third of the three General Creeds. It originated about 400 A.D. to combat heretical teachings. It emphasizes the doctrine of the Trinity and the Incarnation.

There are churches that do not use creeds. These came out of a movement to restore primitive Christianity and the reliance upon the scripture and the Holy Spirit as the sole guide to faith. Such churches are the Christian Church (Disciples of Christ) and the Church of God as well as the Pentecostals. These regard themselves as movement within the Church for the Restoration of Primitive Christianity. The Christian Church expects a confession of faith and repentance from the individual seeking to follow Christ. They believe that the only Creed is Christ. This is based on the great confession at Caesarea Philippi where Peter expressed his faith in Christ by affirming – You are the Christ – the son of the Living God. Such confession is the gateway to church membership in the Christian church (Disciples of Christ).

The list of the Religious Community continues with the Pentecostals, which is the fastest growing religious denomination in contemporary society and the church of God with its many cleavages. There is also the Mennonites (Mormons) or Latter day

Saints, the Seventh Day Adventists and the Jehovah's Witness (Russellism).

The last two named seem to form groups by themselves because of their polity and doctrine. At first they were disdained by the main line denominations but today they seem to have entered the pale (mainstream domain) of people of faith. *The Adventists* especially have extended their reach through hospital ministry, education, and social services, to meet the needs of not only adherents, but people in the community. There is still cynicism about *Jehovah's Witnesses* but they have many members.

Other religious groups and or cults have served the needs of people. One in particular is the *Rastafarian Cult*. This is a group that dates its origin to Marcus Garvey and Leonard B. Howell of Jamaica, W.I. It began with Marcus Garvey's Back to Africa movement taken up by Howells in Sligoville in the parish of Saint Catherine, Jamaica, during the great Depression in 1924 – 30 that left many people almost hopeless.

The 'Back to Africa' movement offered people of the Diaspora some hope. With the advent of Haile Selassie, Rastafarians found hope in the "Lion of Judah" that would listen to their cry. Soon Rastafarianism began to spread throughout Jamaica West Indies, and the world. The "Dreadlocks" worn by them were to be seen and respected. Bob Marley gave credence to the movement with his Reggae Music, which captivated the world. Rastas not only bedecked themselves with dreadlocks, but also opened up the clothing and art industries. They are known for their carvings and sculptures which are sought out by important celebrities and corporations. They have shown the world that religion is not only for worship and meditation but can also be seen in the mundane and aesthetic areas of life.

The smoking of Marijuana is an antidote for the Rastafarian's problems. This leads to meditation and ultimately communion with Jah – a shortened name for Jehovah (Yahweh).

The quest for religion is endless. Faith in the ultimate is always leading to discovery of Truth. The greatest quest is to be attuned to God and this is why man will never rest until he finds that peace. The words of Augustine seem to have an everlasting feeling or pull upon the human spirit. "Thou has made us for Thyself, and our hearts are restless until they find rest in Thee."

Epilogue

In this book I have examined some of the tenets of Religion by employing the disciplines of the History of religion, Philosophy of Religion and Psychology of Religion. Much of this or to a great extent, these disciplines impinge upon the history of Higher Education. This has had a great impact on the course of men's religious faith. I have discovered that Religion is inescapable for man. He is a religious being. He was born in Religions. His actions have religious implications. His quest for God now and for the future depends on religion.

The Living Religions of the world all have a common denominator. They purport to ascertain the whereabouts of the Ultimate. The longings and cravings of the human spirit is always present in man. Judaism will present immortality. Hinduism and Buddhism will offer Nirvana – a place of contentment and utter bliss. Christianity will offer heaven or felicity with God through his son Jesus Christ. Christianity offers eternal life here and now on the basis of accepting Jesus as Lord, and there is a continuation of that life in the hereafter. Christianity is not built on codes and dogma that will lead to eternal life. It is more than a religion that is based on morality. Christianity is built on Faith; faith in a risen Savior and Lord.

As such, Christianity is exclusive. The question may be raised-If one can only be saved in the name of Jesus, then what has happened to people of faith before the advent of Christ, and what will happen to the adherents of other religions since the last 2000 years? Since religion is a matter of faith and since God determines who belongs to Him; then He must make some provision for those who have served Him whether through Monotheism or otherwise. All who don't reject evidence of him (Romans1:20 and Ecclesiastes 3:11) and seek him will find him (Deuteronomy 4:29). This would be true especially for Jews and Muslims.

The Christian Religion existed alongside the mystery religions of the Ancient Near East and prevailed. It offered men the way back to God through His only begotten son, Jesus Christ. St. Paul at Athens told Philosophers and Teachers that "In him we live and move and have our being." (Acts 17:28) In the Epistle of

Philippians he reminded his readers that at the name of Jesus, every knee should bow, and every tongue confess Him as Lord to the glory of the Father. (Philippians 2: 10-11)

While we do not want to lose our identity as Christians, yet we must not be intolerant or belligerent with others who do not share our Faith. Indeed the church in some respects has done just that when adherents engaged in aggressive colonization, evangelism and missionary enterprise. Christianity has been taken to nearly all world cultures. Some missionaries saw fit to disarm the religions that they discovered existed prior to their arrival. Others have adopted the measure of cooperation with the hope that gradually the people will come to accept the TRUTH.

In 1948 (after World War II), the World Council of Churches was established in Geneva Switzerland with the view of alleviating the tension of a war stricken world. This became an Ecumenical movement. Ecumenism is derived from the Greek word 'Oikos" meaning House. The Church therefore has become a household of Faith, living under one roof.

I was privileged to be a part of the United Theological Seminary of the West Indies in my early preparation for the Christian ministry. The students of the seminary were drawn from six denominations: Baptists, Disciples of Christ, Congregation-alists, Methodists, Presbyterians, Quakers. We all shared lectures from the various lecturers and Professors of the Denominations listed as well as worship and Communion services and quiet days that brought us together for prayer and meditation and reflection. I was also exposed to the Jamaica Council of Churches, the Brooklyn Council of Churches in which the Christian Church came together to work for the well being of the community in which the churches had a ministry. Added to this is my Theological, Philosophical training and training in the History of Religion and Education which exposed me to the great minds in the History of Christian thought. These have all impacted me, not just to accept Liberalism. I still maintain my Neo-Conservative thinking.

Since my residence in Florida and through contacts with the Churches, I have discovered a certain wave of Fundamentalism and Sectarianism in the Church. This tends to box people in and label them according to their religious faith. I do not want to fall in the trap of labeling. I believe that faith transcends time and space, culture and institution and rises to praise the Triune God. Only God knows His true servant. Therefore the title of my book: 'Faith beyond Borders' is that by which I stand as a Christian.

I have always been amused when at the National service one leader from the various Religions represented had to say a prayer. Which God is he addressing and who will hear his prayer? It is an attempt at Ecumenism but each faith's view of God is different and they bring to bear different views on how they perceive prayer. We attempt to move beyond borders which are key differences in Faith and practice of that faith.

The history of Religion reveals that religion has attracted some of the world's best minds. These as well as those who are of lesser minds have denied themselves in order to support the Christian cause especially those in the latter category. Christianity has known of the sacrifices of Missionaries, Evangelists, and Philanthropists who have given to the Church their gifts of time, talent and material possessions. They have built churches, cathedrals, colleges, universities, hospitals and infirmaries

From St. Augustine to Pope John Paul II of the Orthodox Church, as well as Non-conformists there has been an out pouring of gifts to the Church. The influence of the Church transcends boundaries whether geographical, political and societal. St. Francis of Assisi is noted for his famous prayer which motivates those who sing it as well as those to whom it is sung – Lord, make me an instrument of Thy peace. That where there is hatred, I may bring love, etc. etc.

Pope John Paul II through faith was able to change the political and moral fabric of the world beginning in his native Poland, then Russia, Great Britain, the United States and the rest of the world. At his death the world leaders attending his funeral service exceeded 200. These included Presidents, Prime Ministers, Princes, Queens, Kings. The number of mourners exceeded the population of Rome and the Vatican.

But what of the unsung heroes of the Faith who have walked the way of humility and piety; the multitude that worship without being celebrated? The Roman Catholic Church is only a small segment of the Church. Protestants have their leaders of Faith as well. We speak of John and Charles Wesley, Jonathan Edwards, William Booth, Billy Graham. These have all helped in the spread of the Faith. Then there is the humble church member, who through their prayers, devotion, dedication and sacrifice has caused the wheels of civilization to turn and harbinger the Community of Faith to praise God today.

The Community of Faith has sheltered and is sheltering the poor, the hungry, the sinful, the outcast, the despondent and hopeless. Indeed this is the faith that overcame the world and this is the fulfillment of the parable spoken by Jesus in Matthew 13: 31–32. "The Kingdom of heaven is like a grain of mustard seed which a man took and sowed in his field. It is the smallest of all seeds, but when it has grown it is the greatest of shrubs and becomes a tree, so that the birds of the air come and nest in its branches." It is to this end that the faith delivered to Saints will overcome the world.

I deem it fit to end this book with the words penned by Ray Palmer (1808-1887) from the song My Faith looks up to Thee.

My Faith looks up to Thee

1) My Faith looks up to Thee,

Thou lamb of Calvary, Savior divine!

Now hear me while I pray;

Take all my guilt away,

Oh let me from this day be wholly Thine.

2) May Thy rich grace impart

 Strength to my failing heart, my soul inspire!

As Thou hast died for me,

Oh may my love to Thee

Pure, warm, and changeless be, a living fire.

3) While this dark maze I tread

And griefs around me spread be Thou my guide;

Bid darkness turn to day,

Wipe sorrow's tears away

Nor let me ever stray from Thee aside

4) When ends life's transient dream

When death's cold sullen stream shall o'er me roll;

Blest Savior then in love,

Fear and distrust remove;

Oh bear me safe above, a ransomed soul!

This is the victory that has overcome the world, even our Faith. Who is it that overcomes the world, only he who believes that Jesus is the Son of God (1 John 5: 4-5). The Faith of the Saints, prophets and martyrs, has kept the Church over the centuries and will keep it to the end of time. Christians realize that they are not alone. Jesus' promise to the Church is "I will be with you to the end of the age." For this reason the Pilgrim Church pursues her way to eternity when the militant church shall become the triumphant church and shall truly understand. Even so: Lord Jesus come. Amen.

Bibliography

Armstrong, Karen. Islam: A Short History. Modern Library: Random House, 2000.

"Buddhism Deities." Chart of Deities. N.p., n.d. Web. 22 Dec. 2013 <http://www.religionfacts.com/buddhism/beings/bodhisattvas.htm>.

"Comparison of Sunni and Shia Islam." Comparison Chart of Sunni and Shia Islam. N.p., n.d. Web. 22 Dec. 2013 <http://www.religionfacts.com/islam/comparison_charts/islamic_sects.htm>

Farrington, Debra K. Living Faith Day by Day: How the Sacred Rules of Monastic Traditions. Can Help You Live Spiritually in the Modern World. New York: Berkley Publishing Group, 2000.

Harrelson, Walter J. Interpreting the Old Testament. New York: Holt, Rinehart and Winston, 1964.

Farrington, Karen. The History of Religion. New York: Barnes & Noble, 2001.

"Holi- Hinduism." Holaka., N.p., n.d. Web. 9 July. 2011 <. http://www.religionfacts.com/hinduism/holidays/holi.>

Johnson, Paul E. Psychology of Religion. New York: Abingdon, 1959.

Luce, Henry R. The World's Great Religions. Editor in Chief. Time Life Incorporated, New York, 1959

Kerr, Hugh T. Readings in Christian Thought. Nashville: Abingdon, 1966.

Klein, Patricia. Worship without Words: The Signs and Symbols of Our Faith. Brewster, MA: Paraclete, 2000.

"Myths Encyclopedia." Mithras. N.p., n.d. Web. 23 Dec. 2013 <http://www.mythencyclopedia.com/Mi-Ni/Mithras.html>.

Pilgrim Hymnal. Boston: Pilgrim, 1968.

"Prayer in Hinduism." Wikipedia. Wikimedia Foundation, N.p., n.d., Web. 26 Sept. 2012. <http://en.wikipedia.org/wiki/Prayer_in_Hinduism>.

"Preparing for Passover." Judaism & Jewish Life.
    N.p., n.d. Web. 16 July 2012.
    <http://www.myjewishlearning.com/>.

Price, James L. Interpreting the New Testament. New York: Holt, Rinehart
    and Winston, 1961.

The Holy Bible, Revised Standard Version. New York: Thomas Nelson & Sons,
    1972.

"Similarities between Jesus and Pagan Figures." Investigating the Similarities
    between Jesus and Pagan Figures. N.p., n.d. Web. 23 Dec. 2013.
    <http://www.thedevineevidence.com/pagan_copycat_mithras.html>.

"Spiritual Mantra." Sanskrit Mantras and Spiritual Power, Vedic Mantra ,Veda
    Mantras. N.p., n.d. Web. 26 Sept. 2012.
    <http://www.ganesh.us/mantara/mantra.html>.

"Upcoming Events." Shaivam.org.
    N.p., n.d. Web. 26 Sept. 2012.
    <http://www.shaivam.org/index.html>.

"What Are Vedas?" About.com Hinduism.
    N.p., n.d. Web. 14 May 2011.
    <http://hinduism.about.com/cs/vedasvedanta/a/aa120103a.htm>.

www.ingramcontent.com/pod-product-compliance
Lightning Source LLC
LaVergne TN
LVHW051249080426
835513LV00016B/1820